I0823013

HOW TO DRAW A TREE

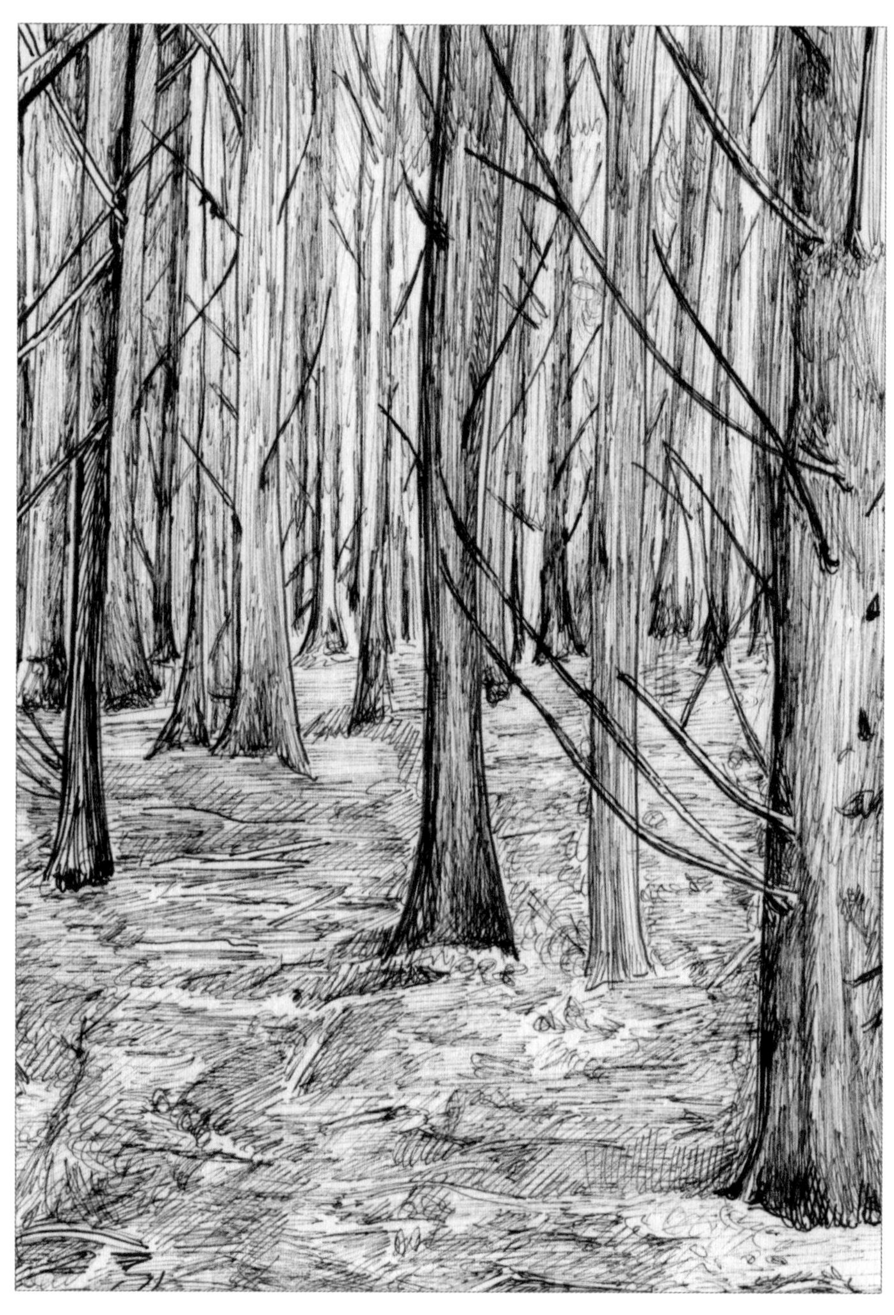

Dedicated to the memory of Joan Ives (1926–2022)

HOW TO DRAW A TREE

From the Fruit to the Forest

ALEX BOON

DAVID & CHARLES
— PUBLISHING —

www.davidandcharles.com

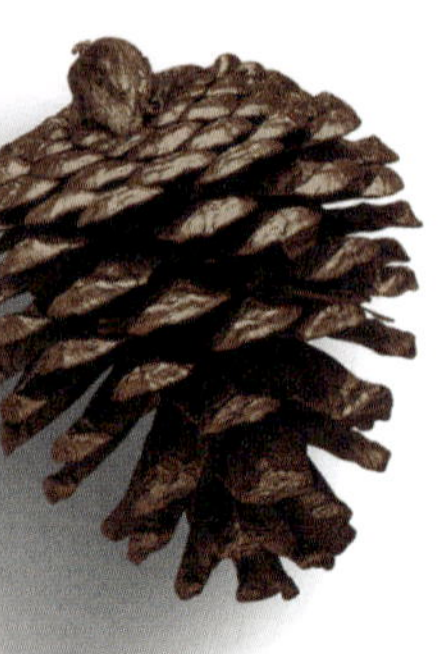

Contents

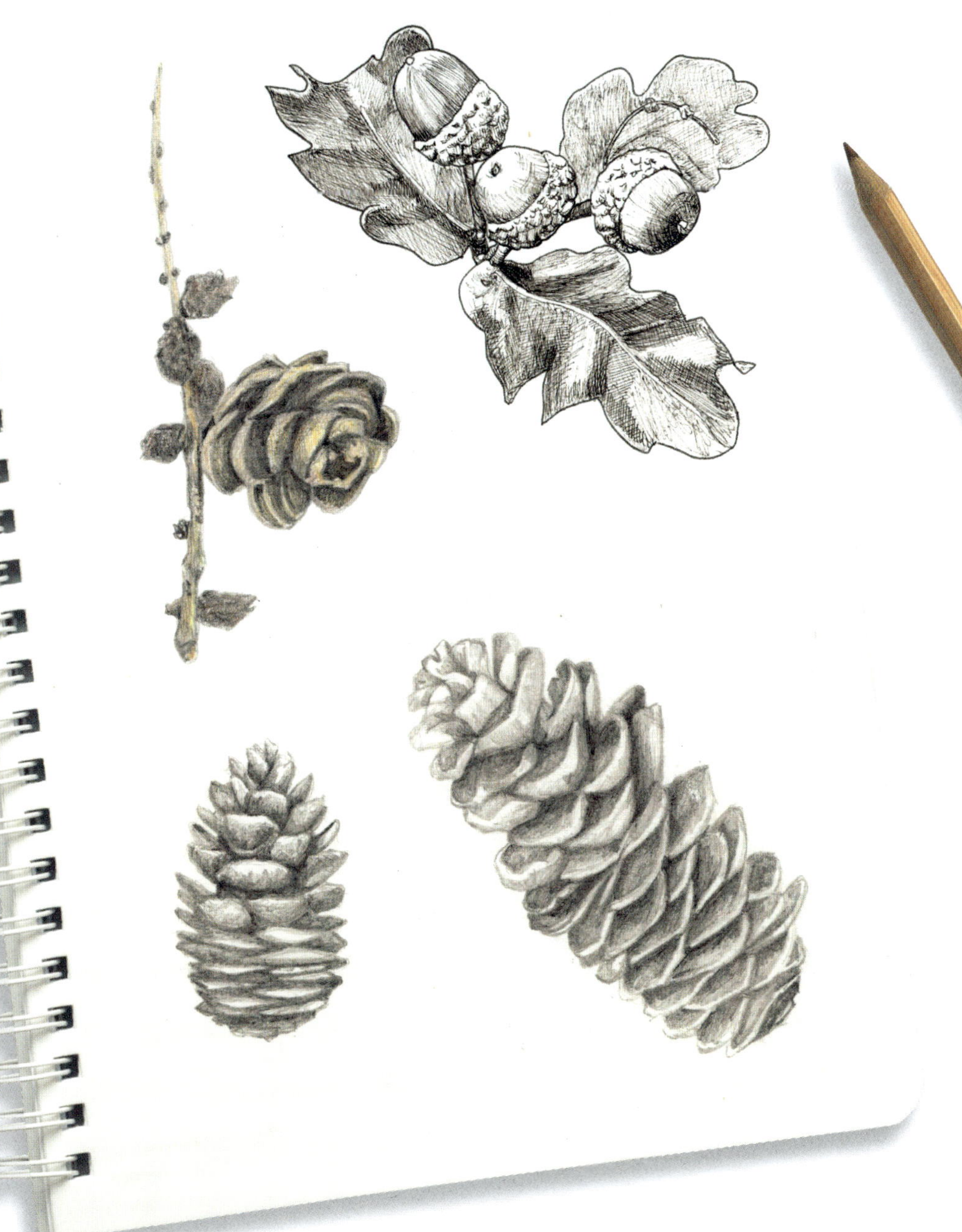

Introduction

The careful observation and creative recording of nature is a passion I have pursued through much of my life. Sketching trees has greatly helped my artistic development, and learning about them has instilled a sense of wonder in the everyday. Watching trees, especially old trees, brings a perspective on life: you are in the presence of elders. It is well known that time among trees is great for our health, and we can give back to trees by getting to know them and caring for the environment they stand in.

Over the years, I have known several special trees that I have returned to draw time and time again. Trees vary through the seasons and, as we sketch them, they introduce us to the world of animals, birds, insects, and plants that they support. We can understand the story of a tree by examining its surroundings and, conversely, we can really come to know and love an area by looking at its trees.

I use a creative method known as nature journaling to explore my personal relationship with nature; it is my favourite way to interact with the world. Through regular nature journaling I have developed my drawing skills, learned to identify different local species, and grown a deep love for my local wild places. I have become a better artist as a result of a concerted effort to observe nature close to home at all times of year.

In this book, I hope to inspire you to document a tree or a group of trees in your local area, whether in a nature journal or just through the pleasure of drawing and creating. I will share a suite of different techniques that you can use to get to know your tree, or trees, and to record the changes that you observe in graphite, ink, and coloured pencil. By following the exercises, you will develop as an artist and naturalist, and come to experience and interact with trees in a mindful and creative way.

These two final pieces were developed from regular time spent outdoors observing, sketching, and photographing trees. I almost always work from my own photographs and sketches of a subject that has inspired me in some way and I feel some form of personal connection with.

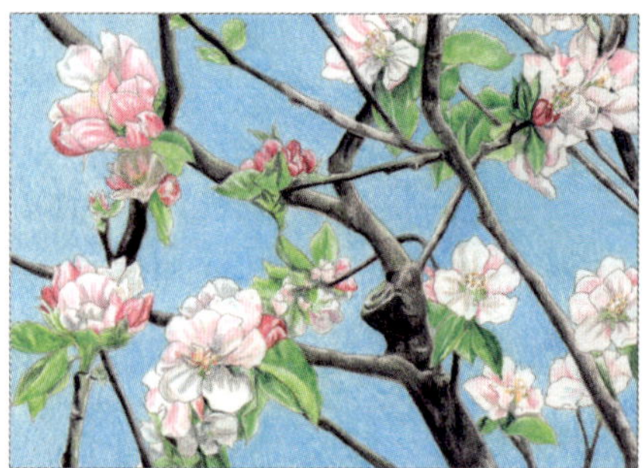

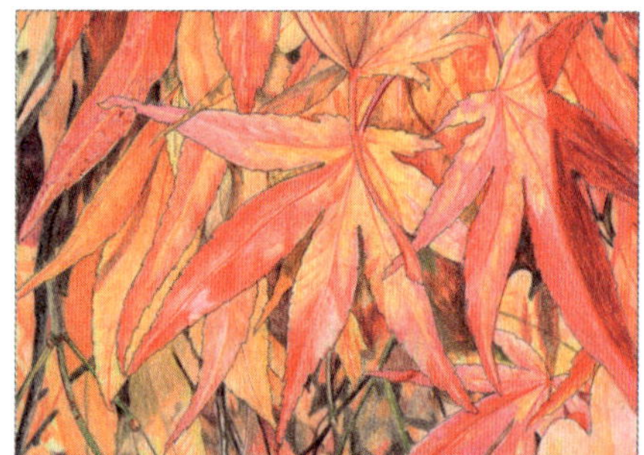

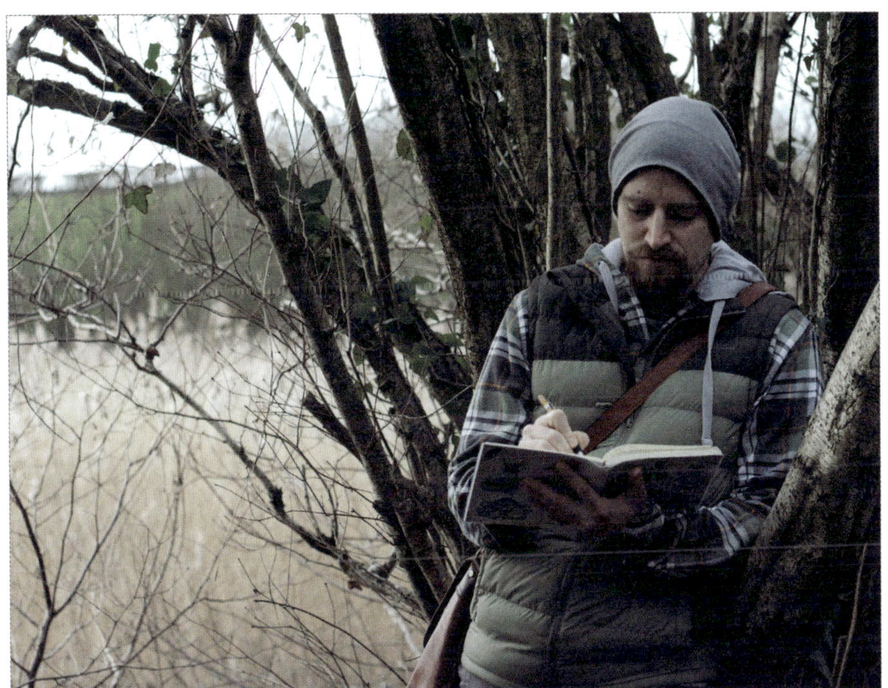

How to Use This Book

This book is split into four chapters, which each contain four lessons using different media beginning with graphite drawing, followed by linework in ink, a coloured pencil drawing, and finally something a little different. The complexity or adventurousness increases incrementally in each lesson. The final lessons in each chapter, and most of Chapter 4 as a whole, introduce techniques that break free of the typical definition of a "drawing".

The chapters take you through getting to know your tree, from its basic structure and overall shape in Chapter 1, to looking at defining features in close-up detail in Chapter 2, and observing trees in more complex groups and how they appear in the context of the landscape in Chapter 3. Finally, in Chapter 4, you are encouraged to reimagine trees through less traditional settings and media.

The galleries at the end of each lesson give you alternative approaches or further examples that will encourage you to expand your practice in different ways.

Getting to Know Trees

Detailed study, observation, and enquiry into a specific subject can be a powerful aid to improving our artistic skills, allowing us to focus on a change in technique or medium. In this book, your chosen tree or woodland location will become your testing ground for developing your creative practice and getting to know your tree at the same time.

When drawing a tree, we must bear in mind that we are always dealing with an individual. Although a tree will be similar to others of its species, no two trees will have grown under the exact same conditions or have the exact same history. Just as a portrait artist will spend hours with a human subject, getting to know them before trying to make a painting of their likeness, we must get to know our chosen tree in detail.

Look at the shape of the trunk, the angles at which the main branches emerge, what shape it holds at different times of year. Looking closer, find out what colour and shape the leaves are, how it flowers or produces seed, what the buds look like in winter. What is it about the environment of this tree that has shaped it into a unique and interesting individual?

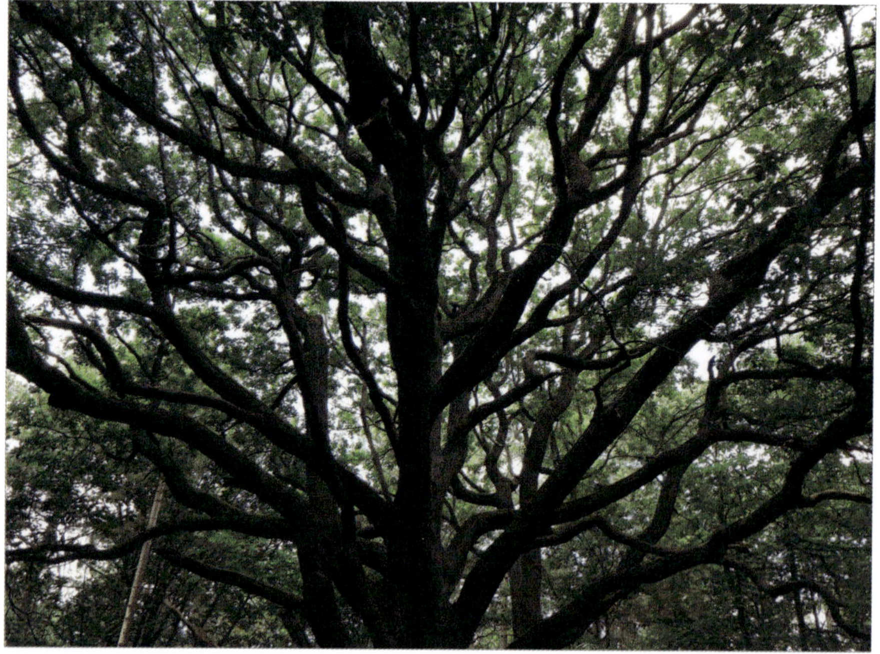

Choosing and Recording "Your" Tree

Wondering how to choose your special tree? Here are a few things to consider:

- **Proximity and ease of access.** *Choose a tree or location that can be accessed easily, preferably during routines that are already part of your life. You do not necessarily have to be able to visit the tree frequently, but it should not be too much of an effort to visit when needed.*
- **A personal interest or memory.** *Choose a tree or location that interests you or means something to you. A tree could remind you of someone, you might have planted it yourself, or perhaps it just has an interesting shape that caught your eye. Perhaps one tree is too small a project for you, and you might prefer to examine a whole patch of woodland!*
- **Having questions.** *Choose a tree or location that inspires you to find out more. Delve deeper by posing some questions, such as "Why have I only seen this tree in fruit once?", "Why is it different from every other tree along this road?", "How are its flowers pollinated?", and "What other species does it support?" Curiosity is a great motivator when starting a new project.*

Thinking how to go about documenting your tree? Why not try:

- **Returning to your tree as often as you can, perhaps once a week or a few times a month.** *Try to see it in all weathers. Maybe visit your tree at different times of day to see it under changing light conditions.*
- **Taking photographs of your tree on each visit.** *You could keep a dedicated tree folder on your computer to click through and help you see the changes over time. You can either draw from these photos on screen or as printouts.*
- **Keeping a sketchbook or nature journal for your on-location and at-home sketches.** *Be sure to record the date and weather conditions each time you visit.*
- **Gathering materials from your tree, such as fallen leaves, fruits, or nuts.** *The leaves can be pressed to use in collages, and the other items can be sketched at home. Be sure not to damage the tree when gathering (see Lesson 16, Gathering).*
- **Using reference materials.** *Learn more about the tree by consulting field guides, maps, or historic photographs.*

Drawing Materials

This book focuses on graphite, fineliner pens, and coloured pencils as the main drawing media. Advice about each of the main media is provided below. When other media are required, extra materials are highlighted at the start of the lesson.

Graphite Pencils

A set of good-quality graphite drawing pencils will be required. As a minimum, have H, HB, 2B, 4B, and 6B pencil hardnesses available in your kit. A good range of hardnesses will help to achieve a greater tonal range in your drawings.

Fineliners

Fineliner pens come in a range of different colours and sizes (nib thicknesses). I recommend 0.05, 0.1, 0.3, and 0.5 in black as a starting point, although thicker pens can be useful for some situations. A black ink brush tip and chisel tip pens are also useful for ink drawings. Sepia and grey fineliners are very effective for some sketching situations and are also used in some of the examples in this book. It is worth buying waterproof pens as standard, even if you do not intend to use paint on your drawings.

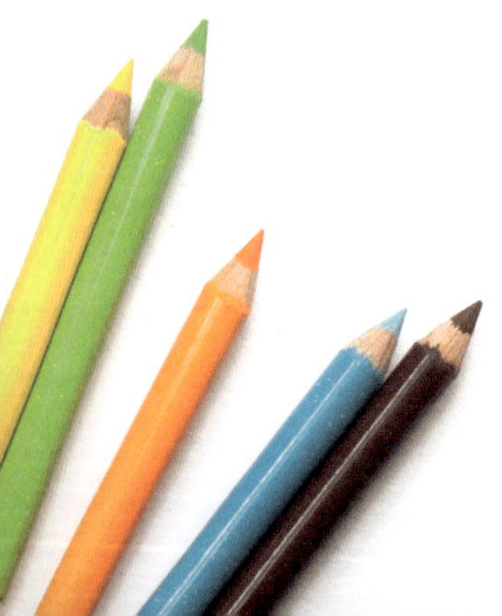

Coloured Pencils

Quality is very important with coloured pencils; buy the best you can. The best artists' coloured pencils are soft enough to blend with but hard enough to hold their form and not create dust like pastels. Good-quality coloured pencils are also more lightfast than student-grade versions.

Paper

Choose a sketchbook of quality cartridge paper for documenting your tree; an A4 (letter) size is easy to carry and large enough for adding journaling notes. However, avoid buying so nice a book that you are afraid to take it outdoors! For projects that you would like to frame or share, use a pad of hot-press (smooth) watercolour paper of at least 200gsm (80lb). Smooth paper is better than textured paper for drawing work, especially with coloured pencils as it allows them to be laid down smoothly and uniformly.

It can also be interesting to use toned or coloured papers. Toned papers provide a mid-tone from which to work both lighter and darker, and give a different feel to a drawing (see Lesson 12).

Erasers

A standard eraser is suitable for most uses; however, it may be insufficient for removing coloured pencil. I recommend a battery-operated eraser or pointed eraser pens, which allow accurate removal of pencil marks in targeted areas of a drawing. A large, soft brush is better than your hand for carefully removing rubbings.

Pencil Sharpener

A regular pencil sharpener is sufficient for graphite pencils, but coloured pencils will usually need to be taken to a much sharper point. Avoid using a knife as it damages the pencil. Instead, I suggest a desk-mounted battery or rotary pencil sharpener of the correct size for your coloured pencil set.

Botanical Materials

You can also take inspiration directly from nature by incorporating your tree into your artwork. Pressed leaves and flowers can be added, you could incorporate handmade papers using botanical elements to emphasise a connection to the natural world, and organic inks could also be created or purchased to provide a harmonious palette.

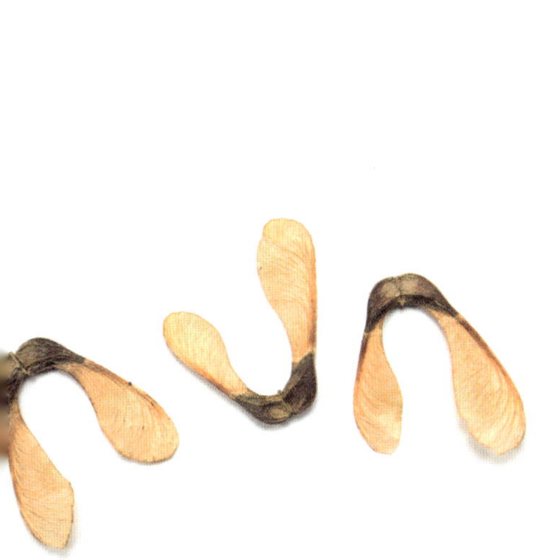

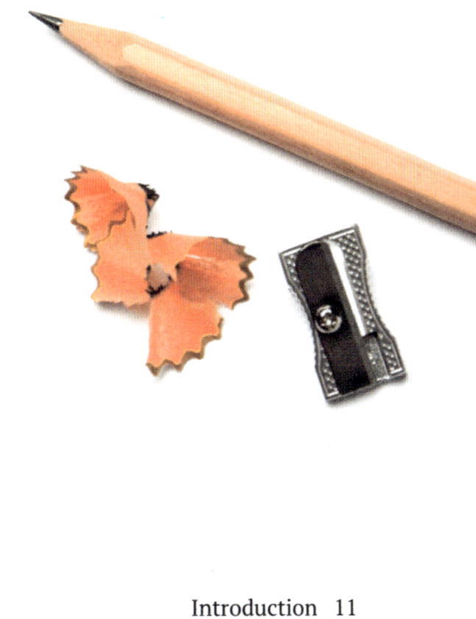

Selecting Colours

Good-quality coloured pencils are manufactured in large and sometimes continually expanding ranges of colour options. The sheer scope of available colours can be overwhelming so, to avoid investing in unwanted colours, be selective based on your intended subject.

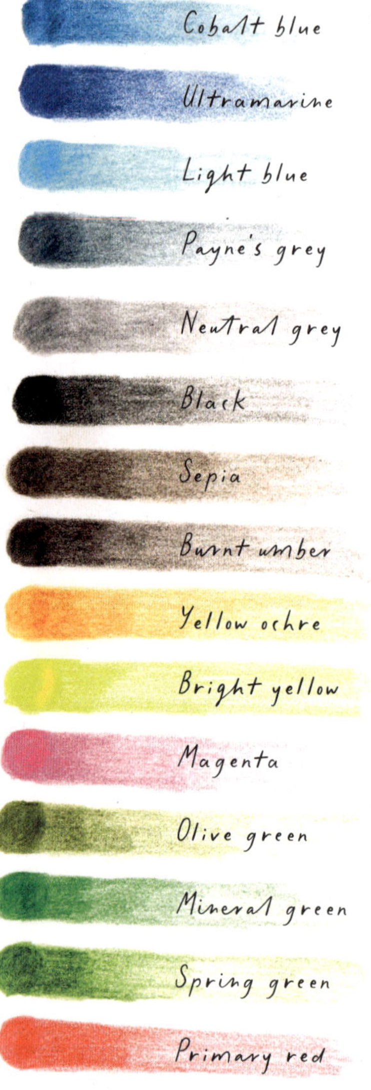

Bear in mind that the colours provided by manufacturers in smaller, pre-packaged sets are often too bright for natural subjects, so suitable colours are often best bought separately. Coloured pencils do not behave like paint – the pigments are not easily blended by a liquid carrier – so it is more difficult to blend a more subtle earthy colour from bright primaries.

As a bare minimum, I suggest the following general colours (names may vary between brands) – you can always add further colours to your set as needed:

- Light blue, bright yellow, and magenta
- Black, white, neutral grey, and Payne's grey
- Olive green, spring green, and mineral green
- Burnt umber, yellow ochre, and sepia
- Ultramarine, cobalt blue, and primary red

Swatch your new colours onto a sketchbook page. Press harder with your pencil on one side of your swatch and lighter on the other, so you can see the range of tones available. Label each colour so you can identify them easily.

Blending Colours

Another benefit of starting with a smaller set of appropriate colours is that you can learn to blend your coloured pencils to make satisfactory intermediate colours.

To begin with, swatch your new colours onto a sketchbook page (see opposite). Press harder with your pencil on one side of your swatch and lighter on the other, so you can see the range of tones available with each pencil.

Next, try blending two colours together to learn how they behave before beginning to colour your drawings. Test your ideas in squares of mixed colours, labelling the combinations so that you can call on them quickly when needed.

Try experimenting further. What happens if you reverse the colour that is laid down first?

When blending, avoid putting too much pressure through the pencil. Layers need to be built slowly and gently to achieve a uniform effect.

Bright yellow + Magenta

Magenta + Bright yellow

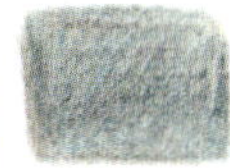

Cobalt blue + Payne's grey

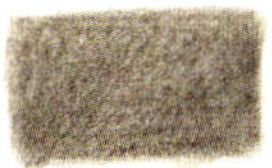

Sepia + Burnt umber

Burnt umber + Bright yellow

Primary red + Burnt umber

Yellow ochre + Olive green

Primary red + Olive green

Bright yellow + Olive green

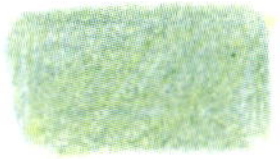

Cobalt blue + Bright yellow

Payne's grey + Light blue

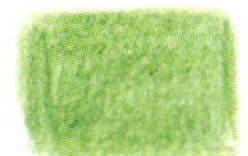

Spring green + Mineral green

Finally, try a simple shape, such as the acorn shown here. Blend several coloured pencils together and attempt to achieve some three-dimensionality using shadows. Further details on coloured pencil blending are given in Lesson 3.

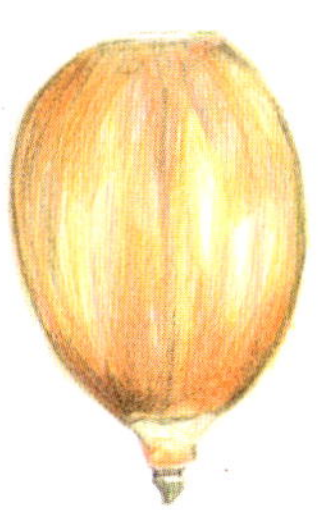

TIP:

Note that there will usually be a bias towards the colour laid on top, so it is very important to build the colours slowly with light pressure. If you press too hard right away there is limited capacity for blending.

Chapter 1

Observing Structure

Starting with the underlying structure of your tree will familiarise you with its shape, characteristics, and relationship to its surroundings. Studying this broader picture is a great way to get to know your tree by examining the structures that make each species unique – its nuts, seeds, flowers, and leaves. This chapter will introduce you to your tree and encourage you to start drawing and filling your sketchbook.

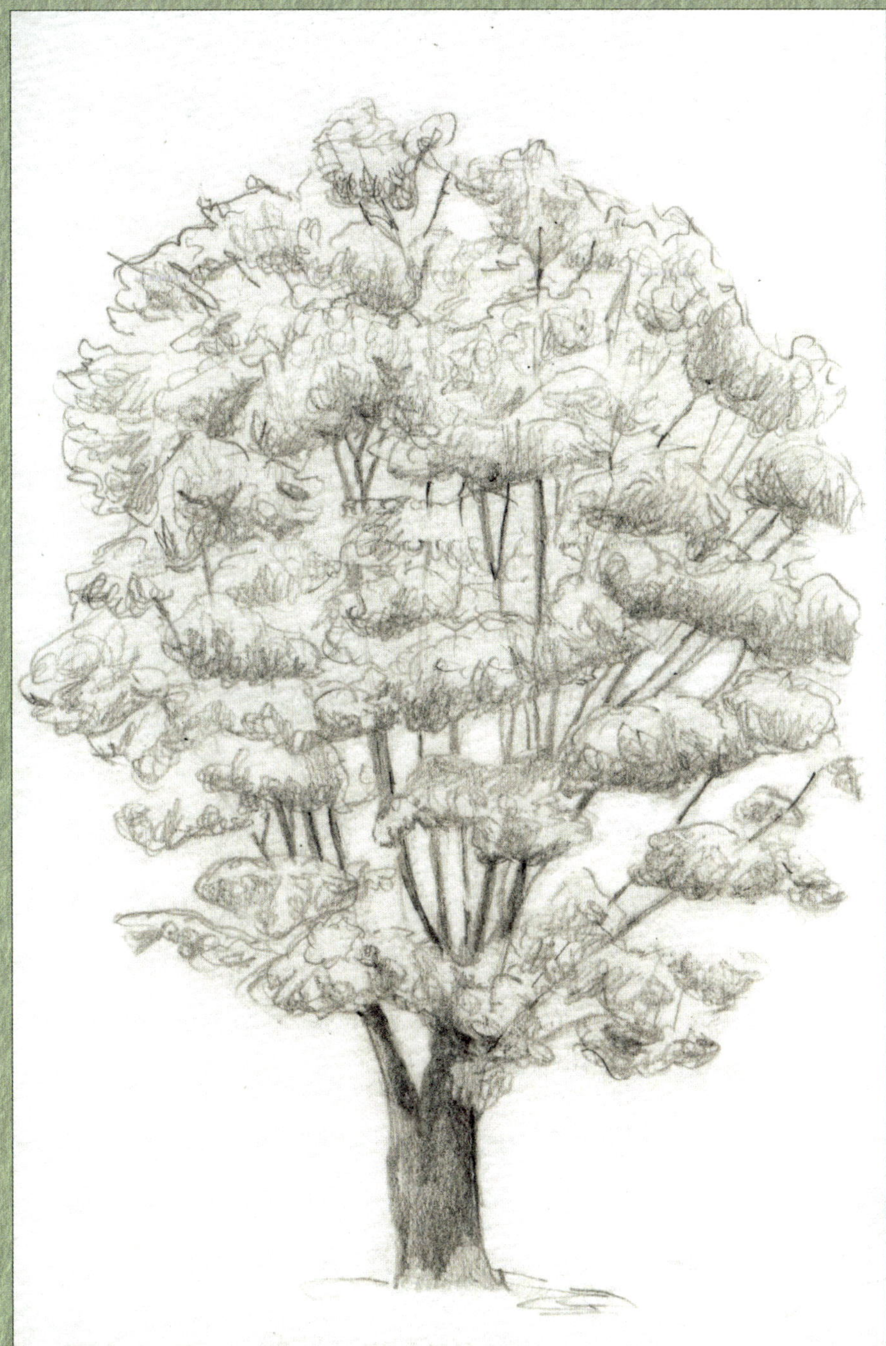

Lesson 1

Simple Trees

There is an enormous variety of trees around the world, but they all share a few things in common. Above ground they have a trunk, with branches radiating from it, and some form of leaves. As with human anatomy, there is great benefit in understanding the underlying structure of any tree we come across. This is why, just as one might begin with a simple "stick man" structure when drawing a human figure, we can begin with a "stick tree" when drawing most trees.

Some trees benefit from a shape-based approach, drawing the overall shape you see rather than the underlying "bones". For example, young conifers, hedge cypresses, and mature deciduous trees in summer have a dense canopy of leaves. However, there is much to be gained by examining the trunk-and-branch structure of most trees, so we will begin our exploration here.

In this exercise, we will look at drawing the structure of two different trees in pencil, one a sapling with a pared-back structure and one a mature deciduous tree with a more complex network of branches. Examine the techniques used here and see if you can apply them to your chosen tree or trees.

Tree 1: Simple Sapling

❶ This young ginkgo tree has a clear branched structure. Young trees can be an excellent place to start when practising the "stick tree" method.

❷ To constrain the tree within the bounds of the page, draw the length of the trunk as a single line from the top point to the base – try to get the angle of the trunk as accurate as possible. Working from the top down, sketch the positions of all branches radiating from the trunk, getting the angles correct. Use an eraser when needed, check as you go, and slowly fill in the position of every branch.

❸ Now thicken the trunk by adding one extra line each side of your initial line. Make sure your trunk is the correct width for the height of your tree; it will narrow as it reaches the top. Note how the branches are thicker as they join the trunk and adjust your drawing, letting the branches taper to a single line.

❹ If leaves are present, it is now time to add some suggestion of them. The leaves of this ginkgo are positioned close to the branch and are relatively dense. What is the structure of your tree's leaves? Are they close to the branch or set away from it on twigs or stems? Observe closely and answer these questions in your sketch. Look for a shorthand for the overall shape of each leaf, ignoring details such as veins and serrations.

❺ Continue to fill the branches with suggestions of leaves until your tree is complete. Resist the temptation to do more to this quick sketch; training your observation skills is the main intention.

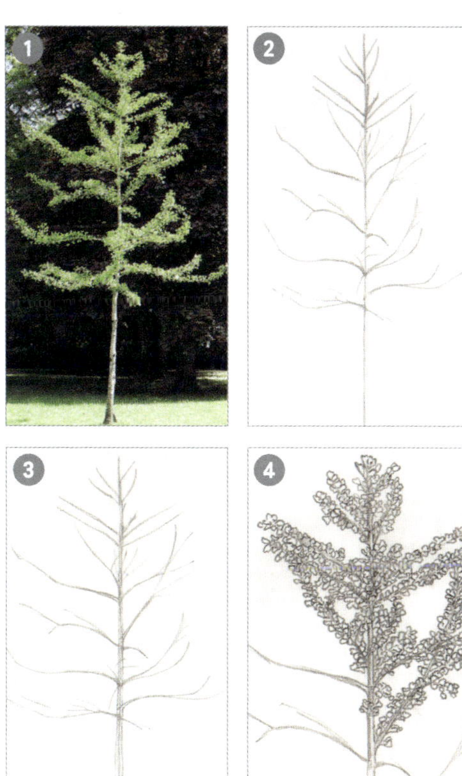

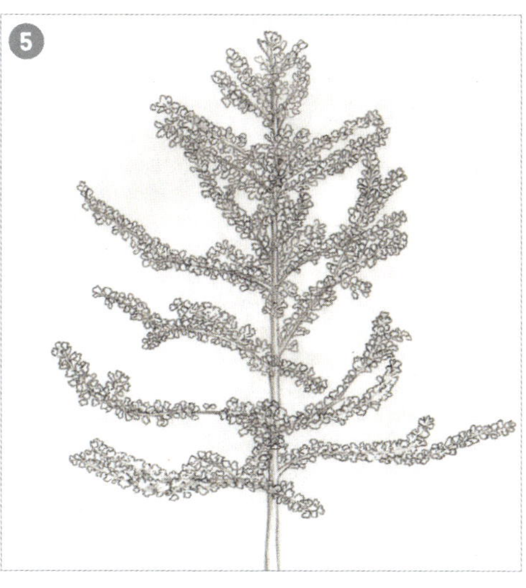

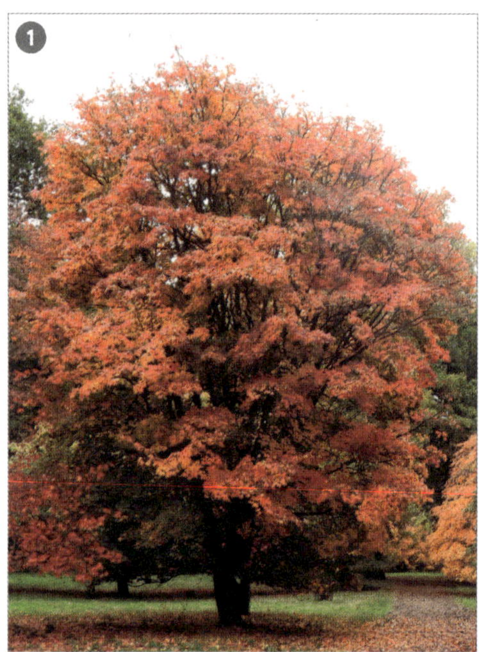

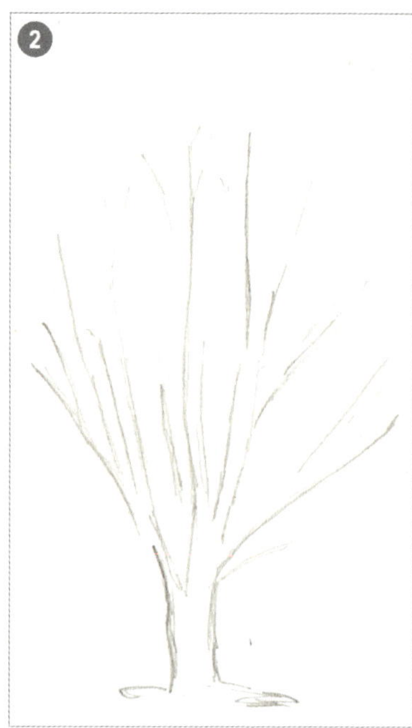

Tree 2: Mature Deciduous

❶ When sketching the structure of a more established tree, the same technique can apply. Looking at this acer, we can clearly see the skeleton of the tree below the autumn foliage. Studying a deciduous tree in late autumn, winter, and early spring can help us draw the underlying shape of the same tree in summer when it is clothed in full leaf.

❷ Find the structure of the tree in line, doing your best to ignore the leaves and focusing on the trunk and main branches. How high up the trunk does the first branch emerge? Measure this distance on your photo and use it to "scale" the rest of the tree. How many times does the distance from the ground to the first branch "fit into" the whole tree? Adjust the size of your drawing to ensure the tree will still fit on the page!

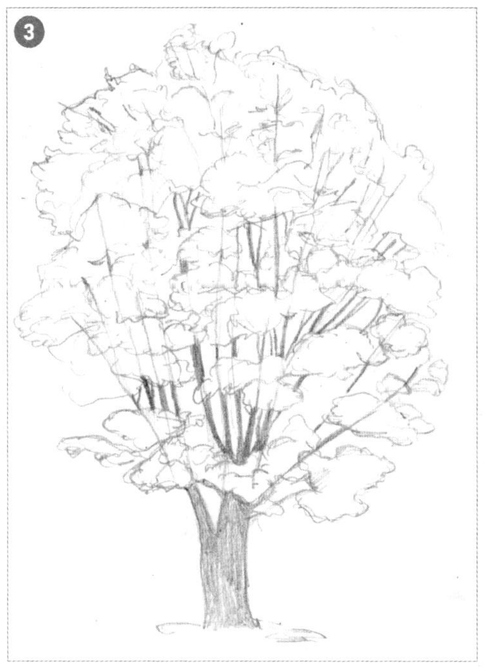

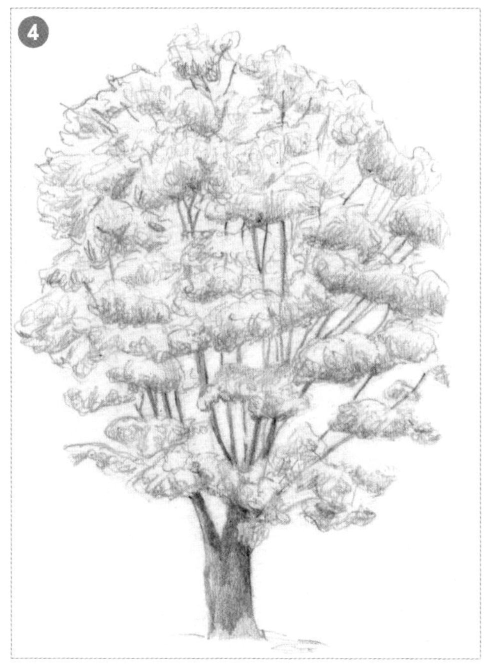

❸ Add in the overall shape of the canopy around the perimeter as a loose line. Now look for "clouds" of leaves. These are distinguished by areas of light and shade on the tree and represent clusters of leaves on the branches. The structure of the tree may be seen in the spaces between the "clouds" so strengthen these lines, and the trunk, with solid shading.

❹ Add some loose shading to the "clouds" of leaves, typically to the underside, following the contours of the cloud shapes. This makes your tree look more realistic by distinguishing where leaves are shaded by overlapping leaves or branches.

Gallery

The exposed trunk of this tall, weather-beaten conifer makes a great subject for a pencil drawing. Denser shading on the inner edges of the main branches and underside of the mass of pine needles adds solidity to the shape. It is a worthwhile exercise to stand near the base and draw the tree's structure from this more unusual perspective.

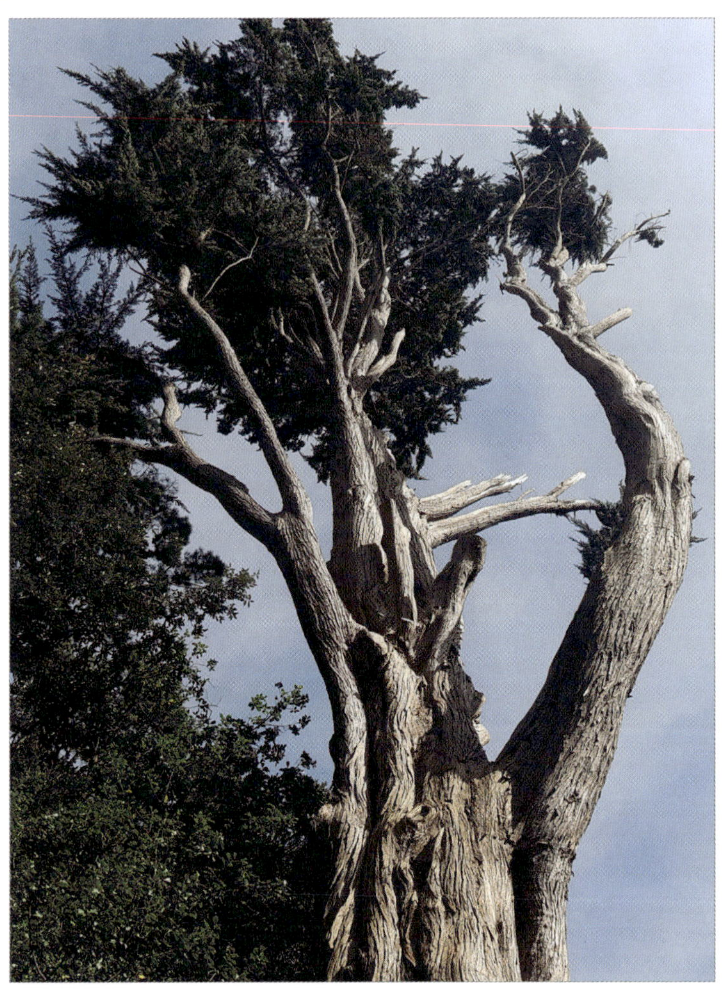

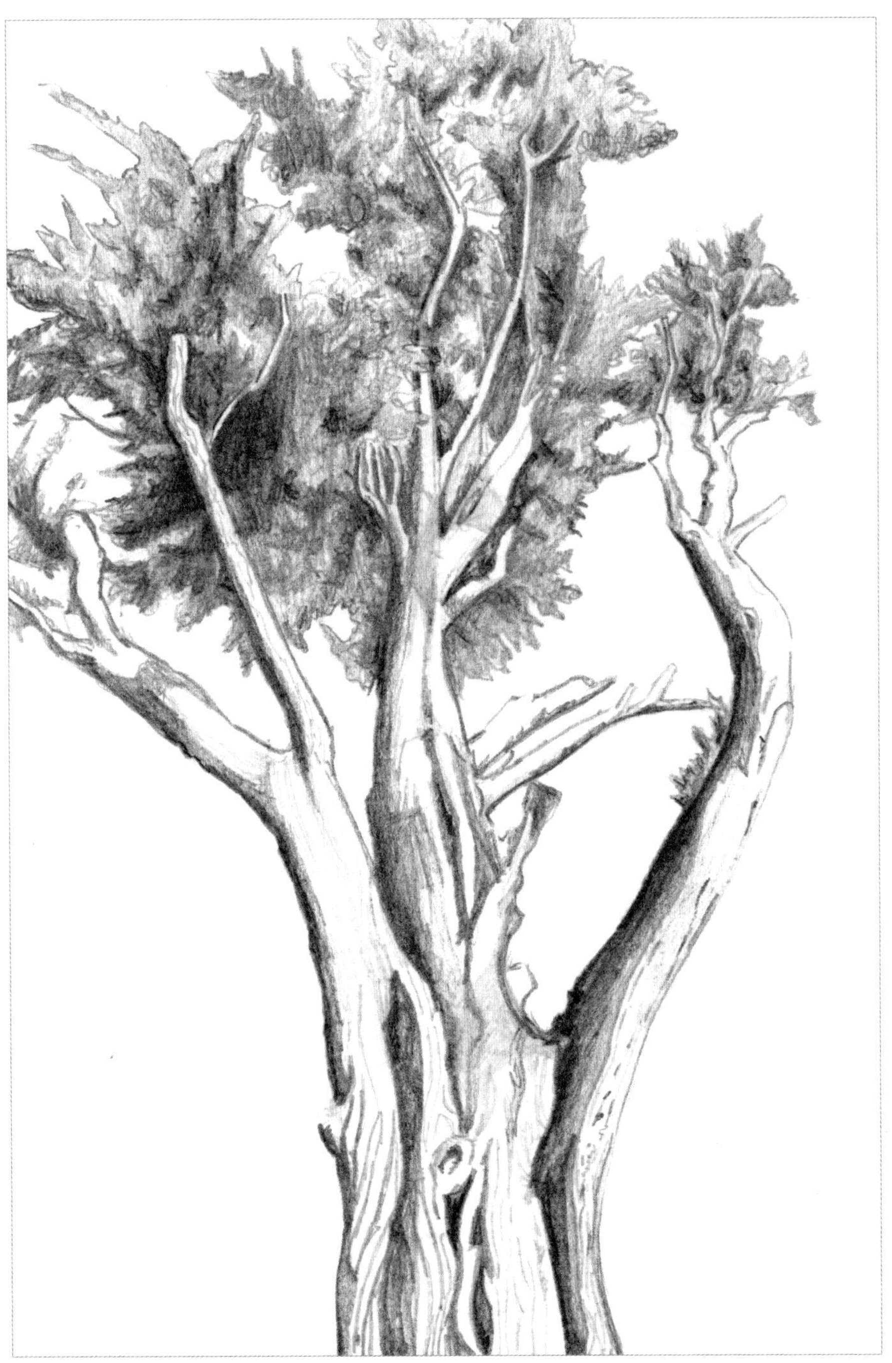

Lesson 2

Nuts and Seeds

All trees will have some method for seed dispersal, which may be in the form of a fruit, a cone, a winged seed, or a nut. Finding these components at the appropriate time of year is an excellent way get to know your tree or group of trees. The simplest of these structures, nuts and seeds, are the subject of this lesson. Here, we will begin with some simple linework, closely observing nuts and seeds through the medium of fineliner pens.

The range of thicknesses in fineliner pens can be used to good effect for building up three-dimensionality in a drawing of a simple structure, such as an acorn. By repeating thin lines in the correct direction, it is possible to reveal the contours of the shape and trick the eye into seeing a three-dimensional object.

In this exercise, I will show you how to use fineliners to achieve this effect for your tree's simple structure. If your chosen tree has a more complex seed dispersal method, such as a cone, you could try this method for the young cone, buds, or a small twig.

❶ You will achieve the best results with this exercise if you begin with the simplest object that you can find relating to your chosen tree or location. I have chosen two examples here, an acorn and a hazelnut.

❷ Begin with some quick graphite sketches of your nut or seed. This exercise works best if you do not make your drawings too large; try life-size or just a little larger. You can fill your page by looking at your nut or seed from different angles, including from overhead and underneath. Remove the seed from its casing if you can, and draw the separate parts.

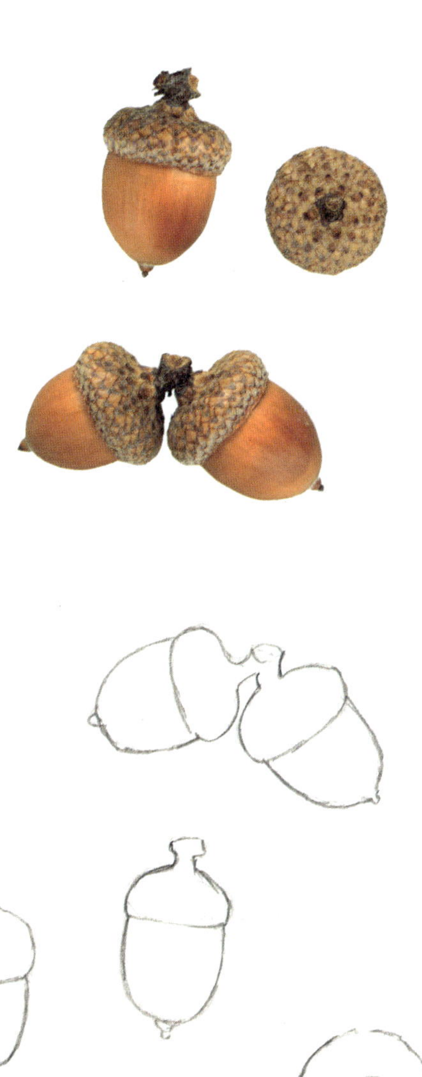

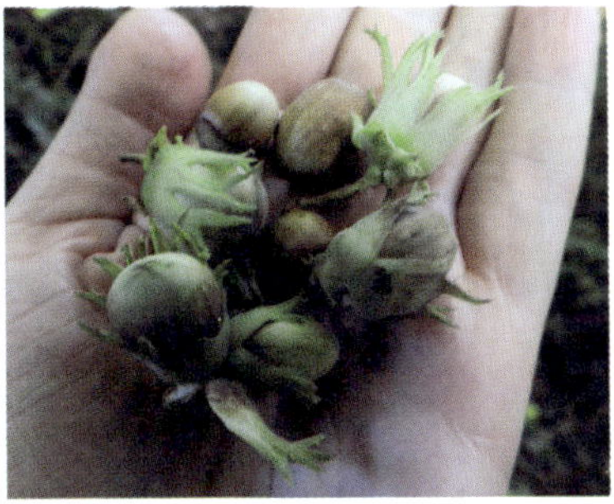

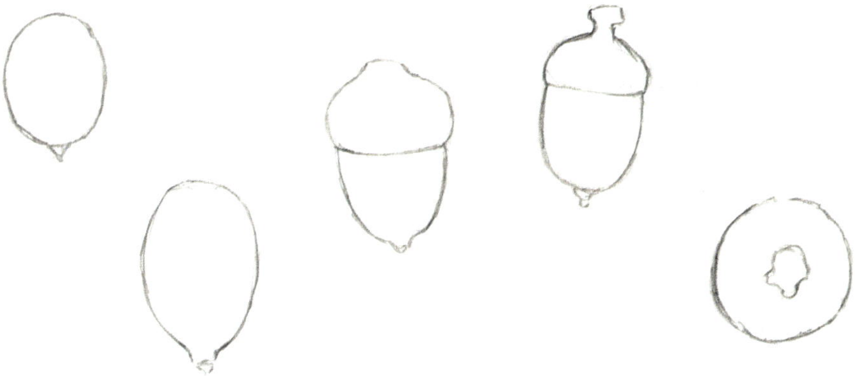

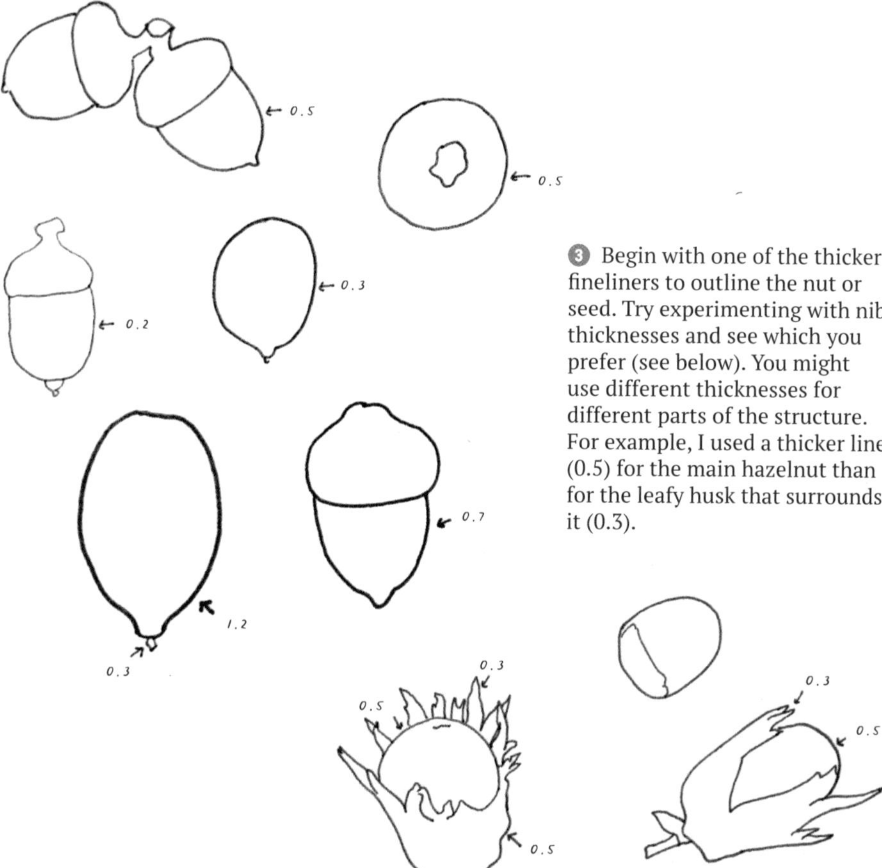

❸ Begin with one of the thicker fineliners to outline the nut or seed. Try experimenting with nib thicknesses and see which you prefer (see below). You might use different thicknesses for different parts of the structure. For example, I used a thicker line (0.5) for the main hazelnut than for the leafy husk that surrounds it (0.3).

Warm-up Exercise: Line Thickness

Chisel tip
Brush tip
1.2
1.0
0.7
0.5
0.3
0.1
0.05

Before you use the fineliners over your graphite sketch, get to know the different thicknesses of your pen set on a separate sheet. In general, thicker lines will be used for outlines, dark areas, and major features. Thin lines will be used to create contours and generate a sense of texture.

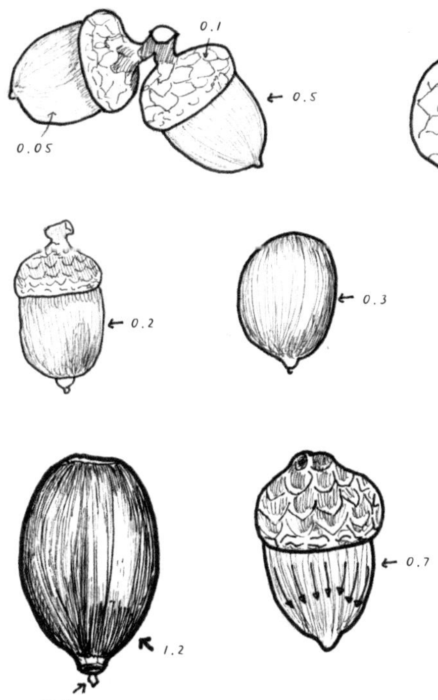

❹ Now add some definition to your sketches and create the internal textures using thin fineliners. Notice the direction of the drawn lines; by curving the lines around the nut, it is possible to make your image look three-dimensional. Imagine you are running your finger over the surface of your structure; what shape does your finger make? For a rounded shape, make the lines closer together at the "edge" and further apart in the centre to improve the sense of three-dimensionality.

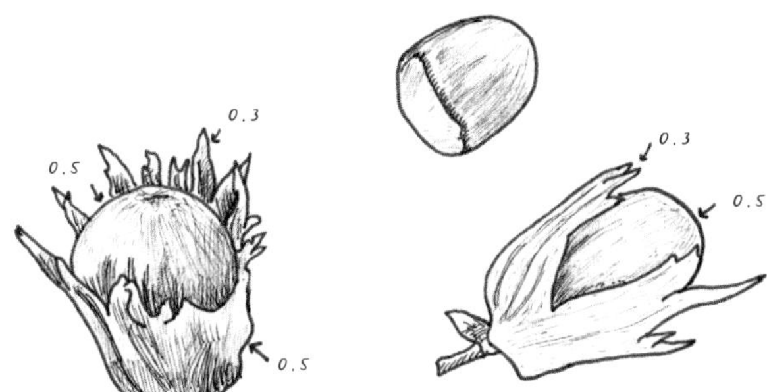

Gallery

You can expand this exercise by including the simple structure in a little more context. Here, I have added the closest leaves to the nut before it is dropped from the tree. This focused observation of how your chosen structure sits in the context of other parts of the tree is important in getting to know and understand your tree better.

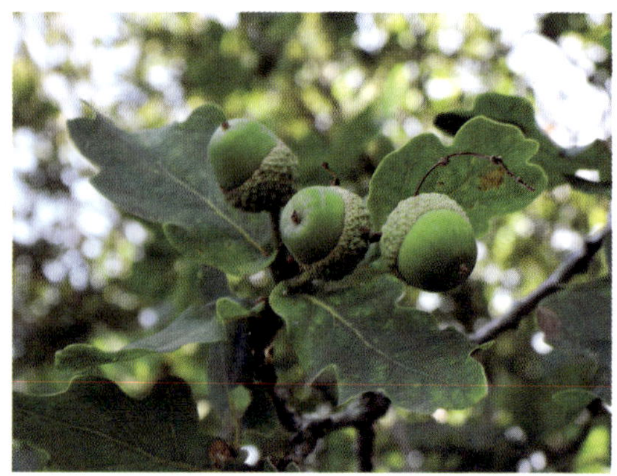

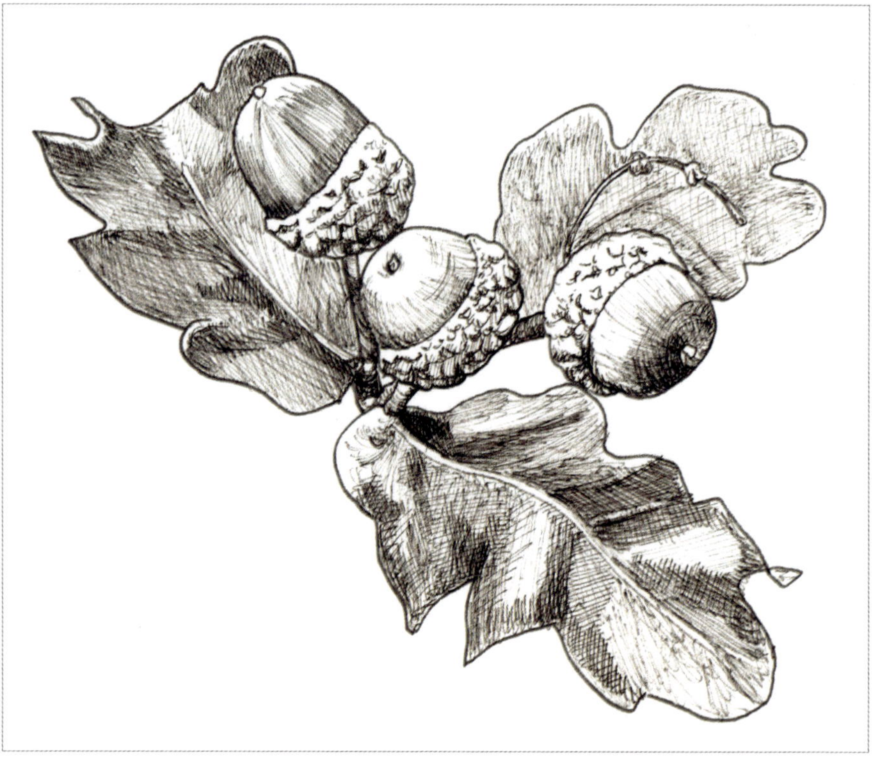

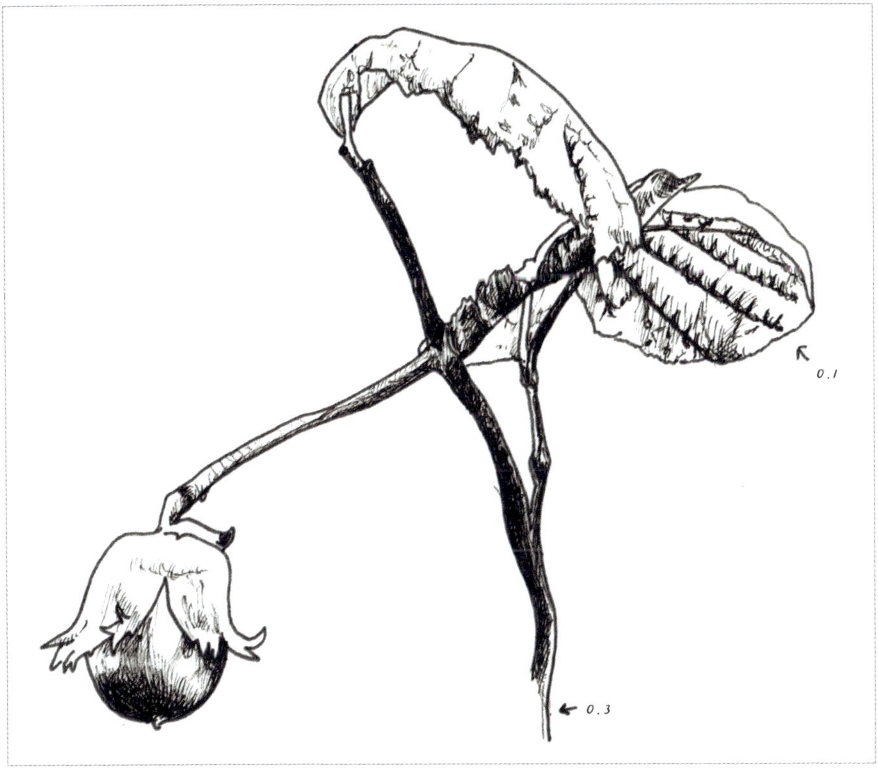

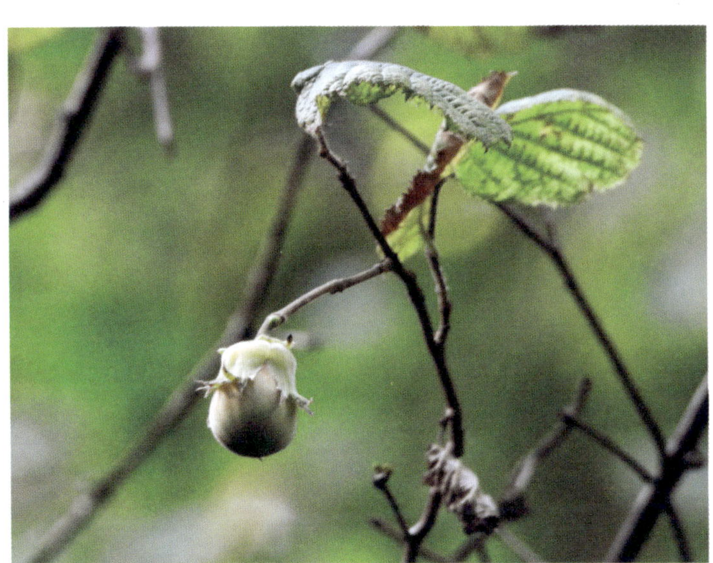

Lesson 3

Fruits and Berries

Tree fruits come in a wonderful range of colours and textures, with often a fairly simple shape to sketch. Some, such as apples and pears, have interesting colour variations on their outer skins, presenting a challenge to the colourist. Others, such as cherries, reflect the light with their glossy exterior, which is fascinating to draw and an excellent place to explore capturing light and three-dimensionality in colour.

Coloured pencils can capture even relatively subtle shifts when used correctly. The most important thing to remember is to allow the layers of colour to build gradually. Avoid pushing too hard with the pencil from the very start, as you might when "colouring in" a colouring book. Instead, fill in areas with colour softly, allowing the pencils to gradually build up in density as you mix and blend on the paper.

A simple fruit is the perfect subject to start practising this coloured pencil technique. Pay special attention to the instructions on colour blending, the direction of pencil movement, and burnishing. The wax carrier of most coloured pencils works very well for capturing the glossy skin of many fruits, giving a realistic feel to your final drawing.

Additional material:

Burnisher pencil

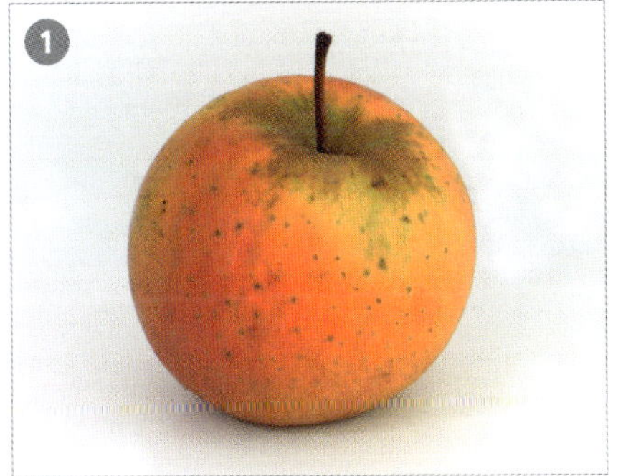

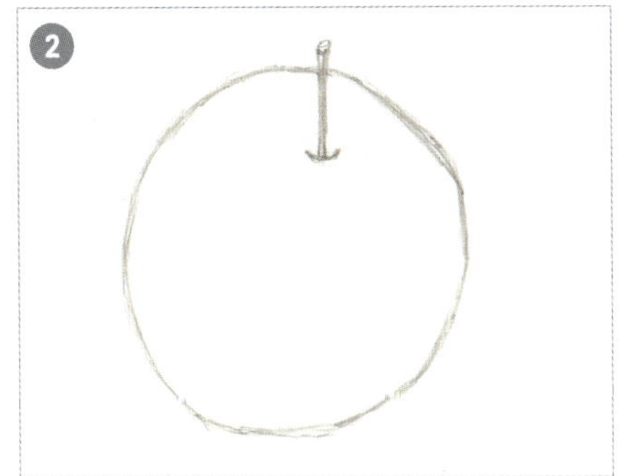

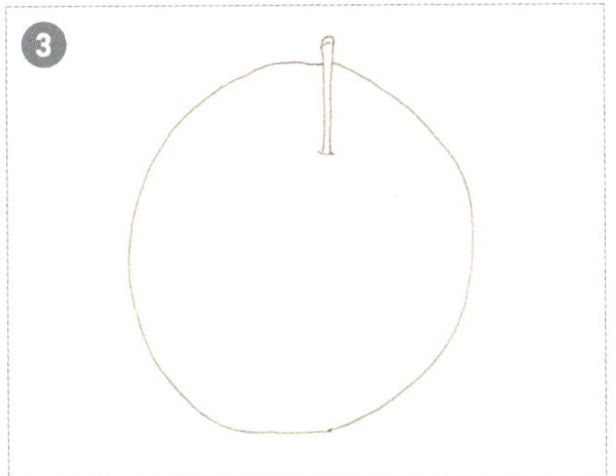

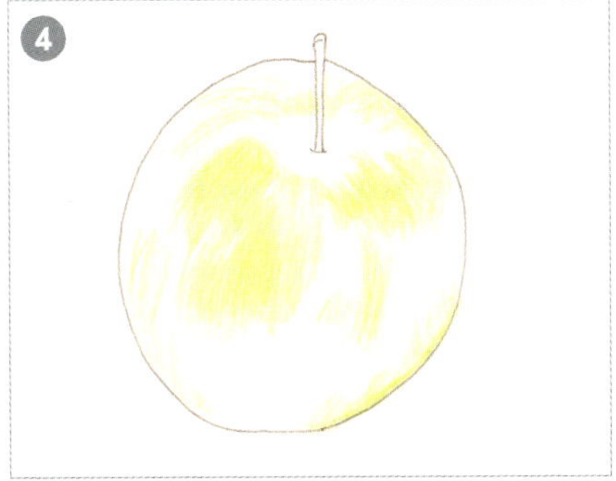

1 Find a tree fruit to work from or, for practice, raid your fridge or fruit bowl for a suitable specimen if your tree is not fruit-bearing or it is the wrong time of year. Look for a fruit that has an interesting variety of colours, such as this apple. You can then expand these techniques to the seeds, nuts, or fruit of your chosen tree.

2 Begin with a quick graphite sketch of the shape. If a stalk is present, take care to position it correctly in relation to your viewpoint. It can feel much easier to work from a photograph, as the perspective will not change as you move your head. However, there is much to be gained from sketching from life – just try to maintain the same position and viewpoint as you make this initial outline.

3 If you wish, use a fineliner to give a final outline of your fruit and then erase the pencil lines. Alternatively, use an eraser to "knock back" the pencil lines, removing any extra lines and leaving only a faint outline of the fruit. Your drawing will be more effective if the graphite pencil line is only a soft guide, as you will add coloured pencil over the top.

4 Examine your fruit in detail and set out the colours you think you will need. Make sure your pencils are sharp. Remember that you can blend colours together (see Introduction: Blending Colours); you may not have every colour you need as an individual pencil. First, choose the lightest colour, in this case a pale yellow, and gently lay this down everywhere that colour appears.

5 Now choose your next-lightest colour, in this case a pale orange. In some places layer this over the top of your previous colour and in others add the colour alone or leave the previous colour to show through. By layering softly, not pressing too hard, you will be able to build up realistic combinations of colour. Note the direction of the lines in this sketch – just like with the fineliners in Lesson 2, if you lay in colour following the contours of the fruit, you can achieve more realistic effects.

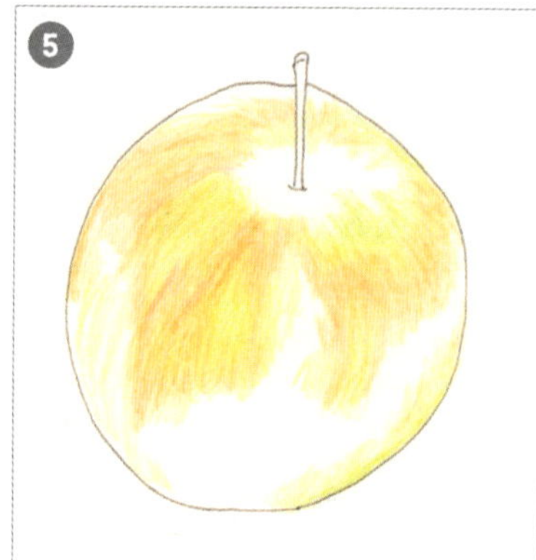

6 Continue to build up layers of colour. In this example, I added a light pink after the orange, and finally a much darker red. As the layers build, the "waxiness" of the drawing will increase and the paper will cease to show through. When you reach this "waxy" coating, your drawing is done and it will be more difficult to add more colours over the top. You can reach this stage sooner if desired (for example, in areas of highlight) by using a special "burnisher" pencil (see Burnishing, below) or by colouring over lighter areas of the drawing with a light colour such as a skin tone, rose pink, or white.

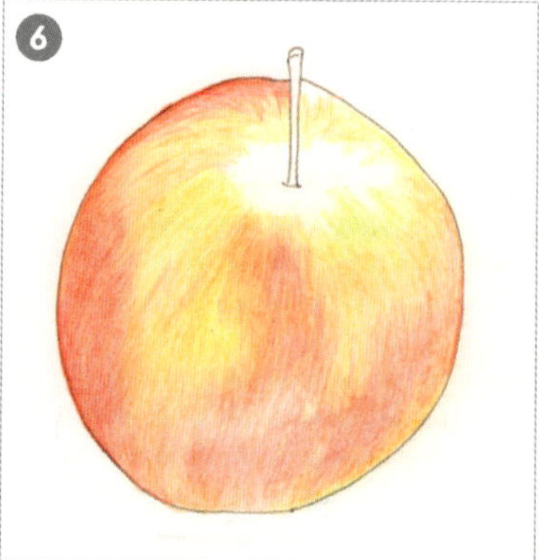

Burnishing

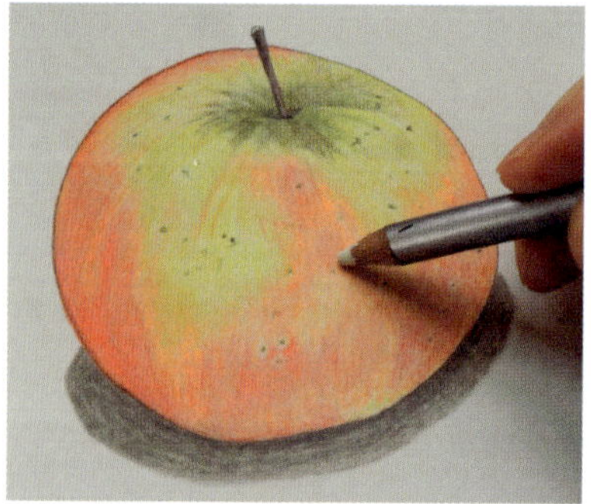

Burnishing is a technique that uses pressure to create a smooth, glossy surface by blending the coloured pencil pigment and wax together. You can use a special colourless burnisher pencil to help – just keep colouring over the area gently until you get the level of blending or gloss that you want and less paper shows through.

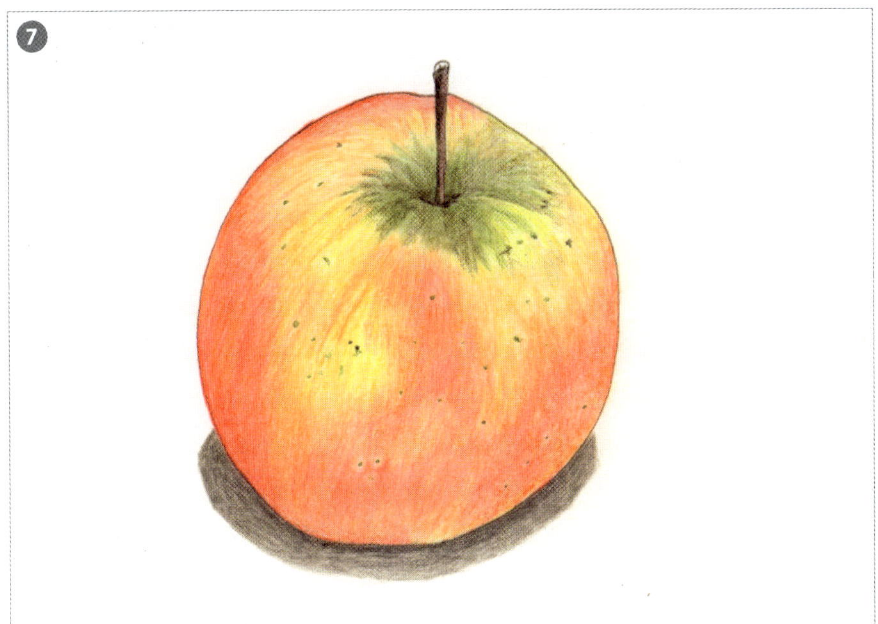

❼ Once you have completed colouring the main body of the fruit, add in the detail of your stem, stalk, or branch, if present, and perhaps consider adding a shadow. You can also add small blemishes on the skin with a sharp pencil at this stage. Finally, give your drawing a layer of “burnisher” pencil or a light colour from your set, to blend the colours together, remove areas of paper showing through, and give your fruit a glossy finish.

Gallery

As an expansion of this exercise, try to look at fruit in the context of its position when growing on the tree. First, I drew the two main cherries in the same way as Lesson 3 and then coloured in a soft background, incorporating the tree leaves. I achieved a softer effect for the background leaves and cherries by using lighter colours, a lower level of detail, and burnishing less heavily than in the two foreground cherries.

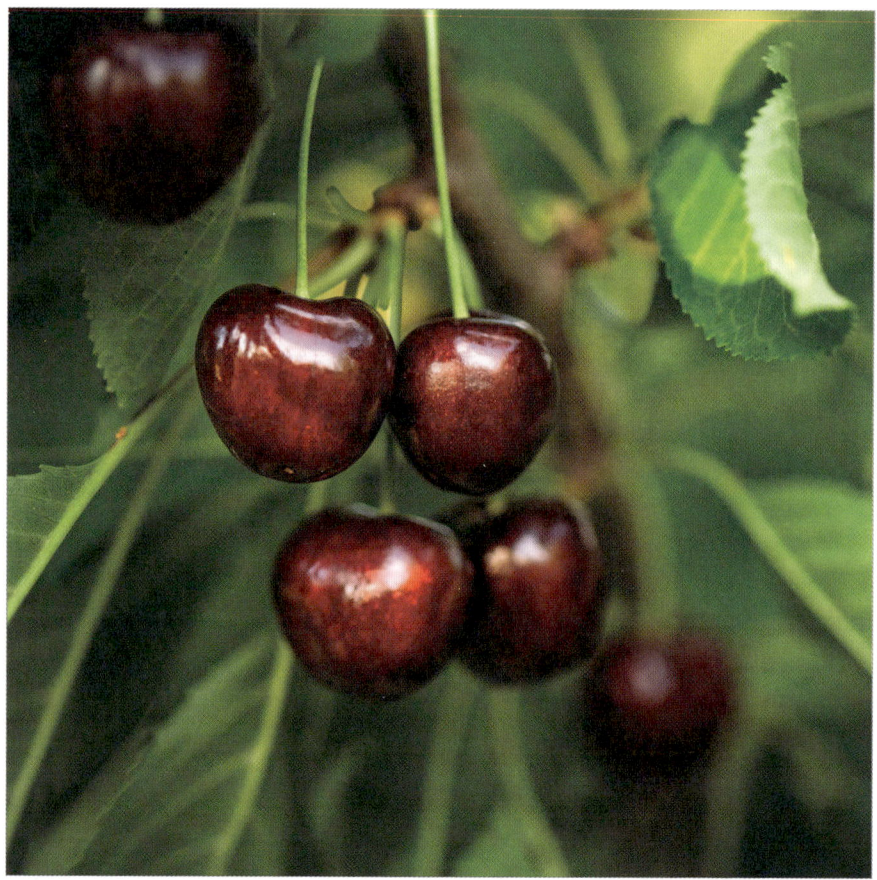

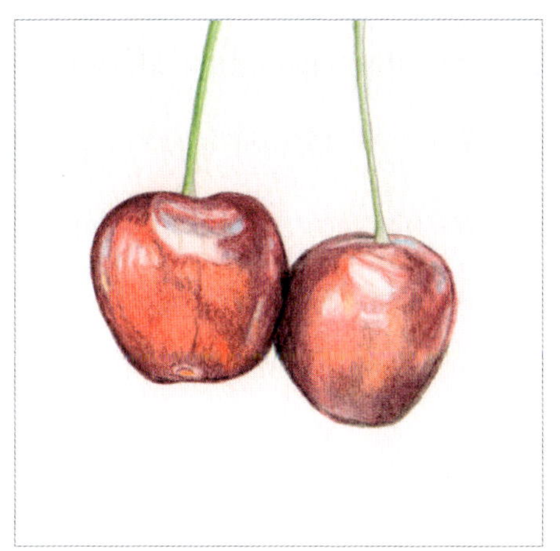

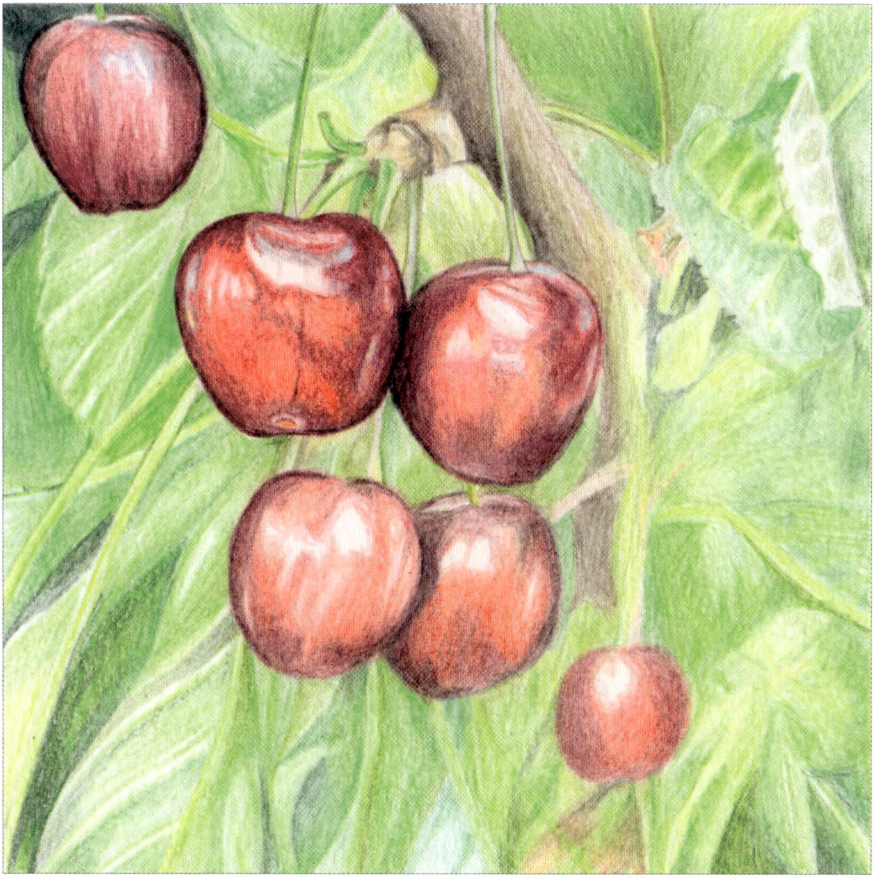

Lesson 4

Notes and Sketches

When embarking on your tree project, making regular notes and sketches is a wonderful way to discover more, whether for a single tree or a group. Your sketchbook might take the form of observation at different times of year, or include your own research about the natural history of your tree and its inhabitants. Become interested not just in the tree itself but the life that surrounds it, and note how it all changes over time.

Keeping a nature journal is an excellent way to get to know your tree or location in this intimate way. Nature journaling is the combination of different types of observation – words, sketches, species lists, pressed leaves, and more – into a single location such as a sketchbook. You can examine the tree from the small scale (the mosses on its bark) to the large scale (a sketch of how the tree fits into the wider habitat around it).

For this tree project, your nature journal could take many forms and I encourage you to be as creative as you can. The exercises below are just examples: any type of documentation of your relationship with the tree or its location can be a part of your nature journal.

1 If you can, set yourself up outdoors with your chosen tree (1a). Take reference photos and start with an overall sketch. I did a quick sketch of my chosen tree in a black ballpoint pen (1b). If you are outdoors, write down anything else you notice – the weather, any birds, or other details about the tree such as its bark texture and whether it supports other plants or fungi on its trunk or roots. Don't forget to write the date and time of each visit.

2 Using your photos, look for some other areas of interest to sketch. I have zoomed in to an area of my quick pen sketch and used a photo to do a more detailed drawing of that part of the tree. I used a "diagram" effect here, using a circle drawn in fineliner to indicate that I have magnified the image. It can be effective to try a different technique or media for each area of interest; for example, I switched to coloured pencil for my sketch of the leaves.

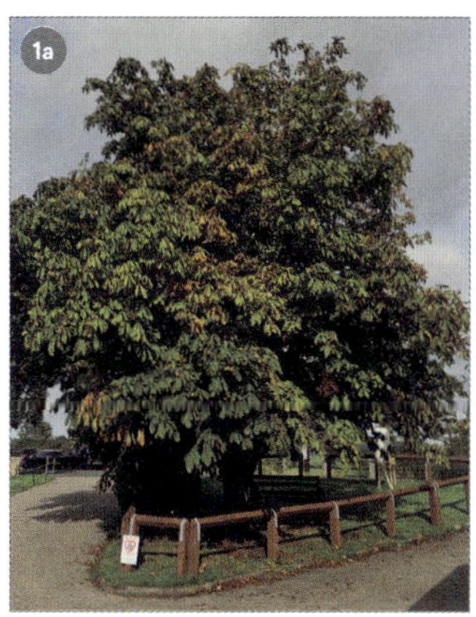

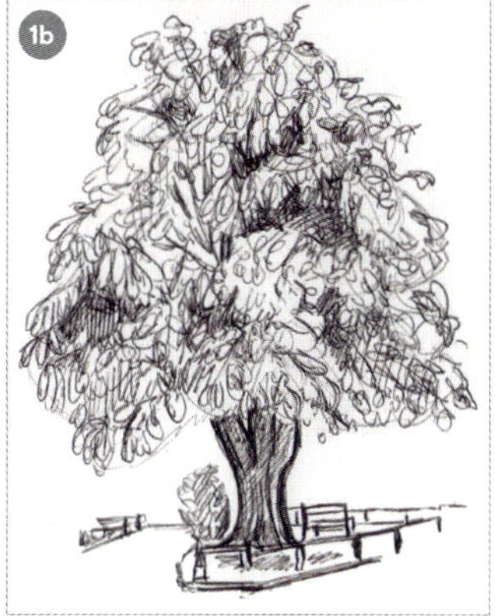

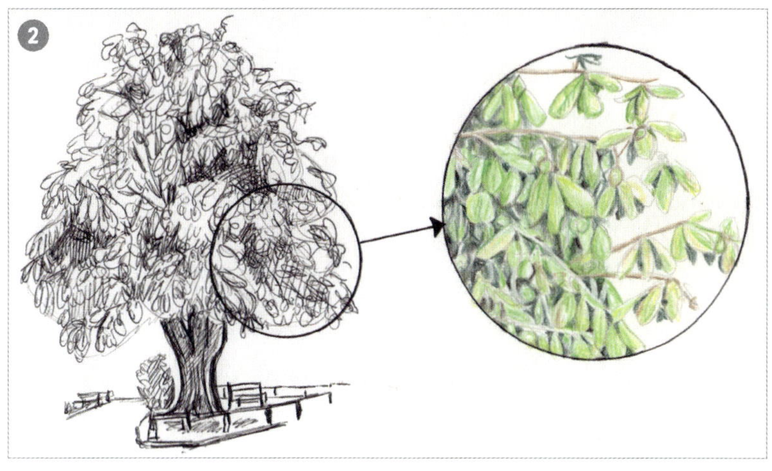

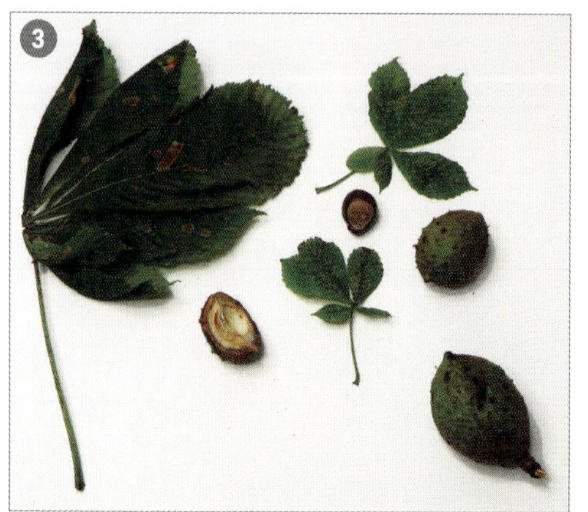

HORSE CHESTNUT

Aesculus hippocastanum

This specimen sits on a small, fenced green by the roadside

Leaves subject to many leaf-miner parasites and other diseases

Spiny green capsules with conkers inside.

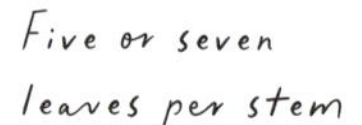

❸ Gather supporting materials to help you get to know your tree. You might take a green leaf, some fallen seeds or nuts, or fallen leaves to press. It is also worthwhile taking photos of your tree at different times of year, making a repository of images to sketch from, collage, or print and stick into your sketchbook.

❹ Use samples or photos to help you track the status of the tree through the seasons. You might use photos to draw the flowers, or gather samples of nuts, fruits, or seeds. Look at the flower or seed casing from different angles. In these sketches, I broke down the horse chestnut nuts and husks into different parts and drew them from a range of viewpoints.

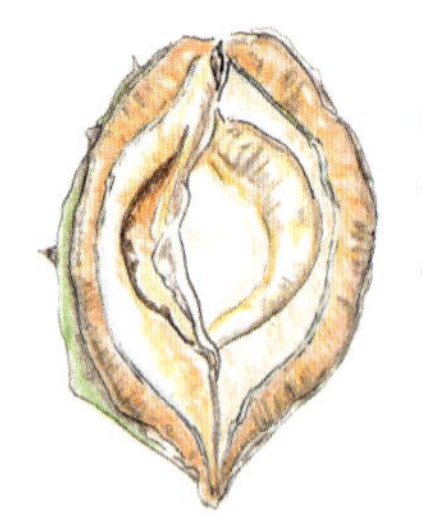

Here is the inside of the pithy husk

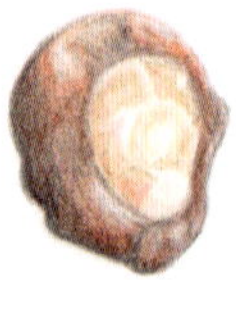

Glossy conkers give the tree its American name, "Buck Eye"

Enjoy the View

Nature journaling is a remarkable tool for wellbeing, especially when done outside. Try to make visiting your tree a regular habit, taking your sketchbook with you, if possible. The nature journal is your place to respond to your subject in your own personal way and works best when you express yourself creatively as you find out more.

Even if you write just a few notes each visit or do a quick sketch, this will help take your mind away from the clamour of day-to-day tasks for a few moments, while being creative and getting some fresh air, too.

Try writing a list of all the things you notice in a quick ten minutes with your tree. Think about textures, colours, and shapes. Travel through the senses and notice the feel of your tree's bark, its scent, and the sounds of the birds nearby. Allow yourself to get closer and closer to all these little details.

See Nature Journaling, at the end of the book, for some more techniques to try.

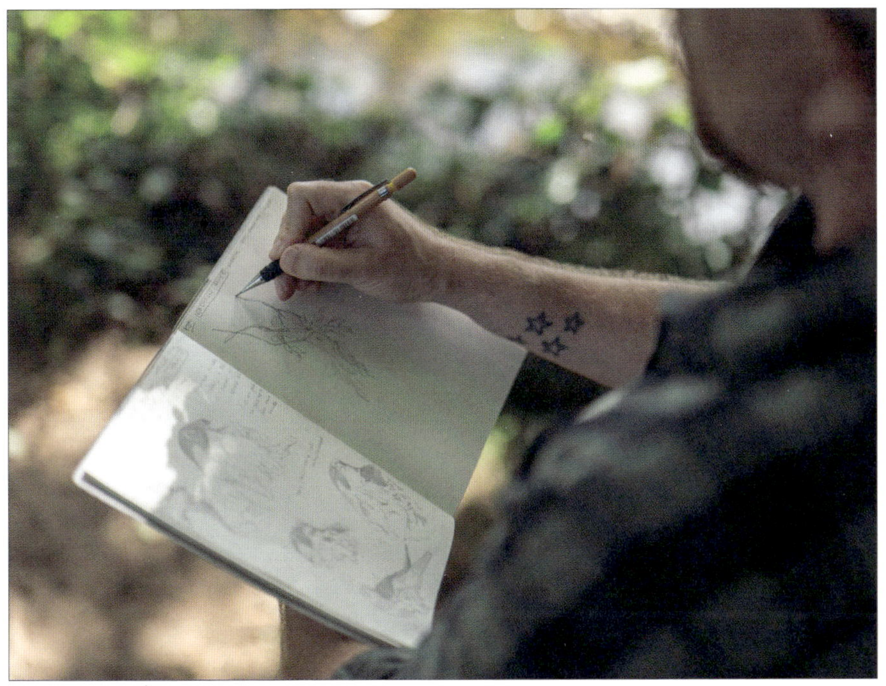

Gallery

In these two nature journal pages, I gathered together photographs or samples from a number of different plants and fungi that were present in the woodland. With a varied selection, think about how you might like to combine text and images together. For my journal pages, I have left plenty of space for some writing around my coloured pencil drawings. To incorporate text, you could keep a diary of your visits to the tree or make a list of the species that you found, to help you identify them again.

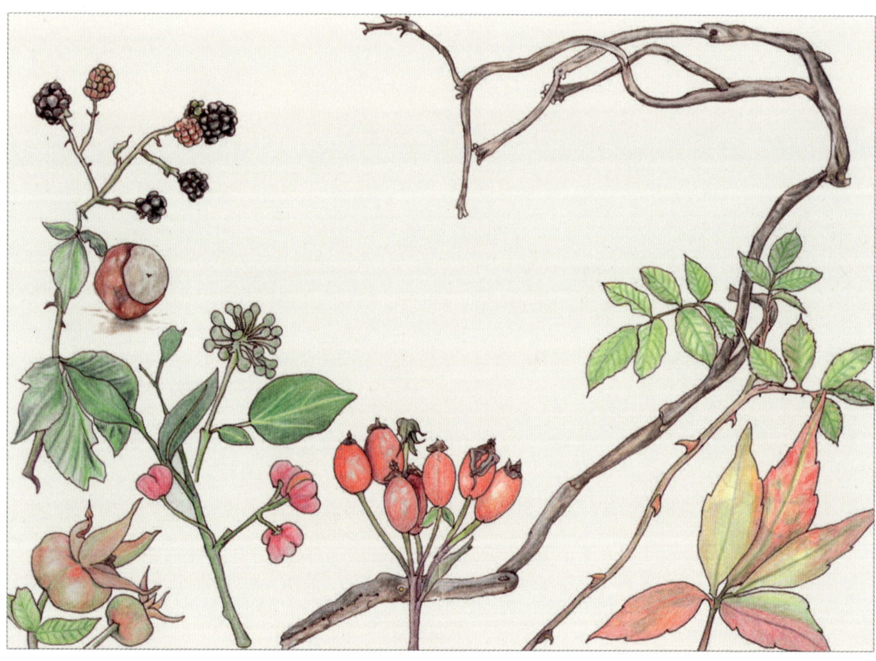

TIP:

When designing a nature journal page, try using several photographs and combining them together into a composite image. Six different photographic references were used to produce the fungi page in the image below. First draw the main subjects of each photo (each mushroom in this case), and then consider how you might fill in the "gaps" between them, perhaps incorporating some of the backgrounds of each photo. This is a great way to use the information you gather from nature journaling and from observing the natural world more closely. Over time, you will develop an understanding of how environments look and this will translate into more realistic "imaginary" compositions.

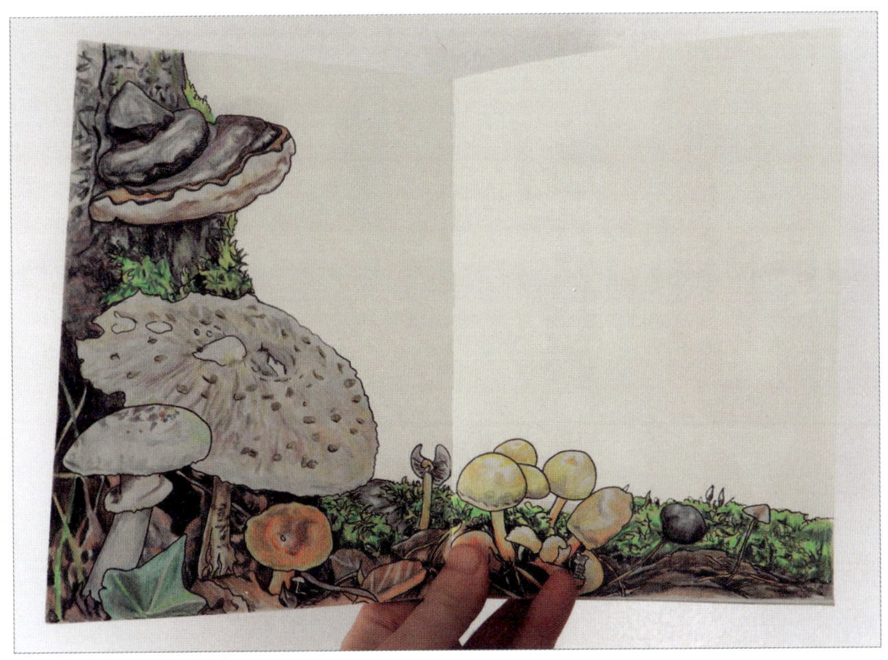

Chapter 2

Building Detail

Now that you have got to know your tree's shape and individual characteristics, this chapter focuses on looking at the more complex details that give each tree its unique structure. With studies in graphite and ink that focus on techniques for conveying tone, and an exploration of colourful blossoms, there's plenty to keep you sketching throughout the year.

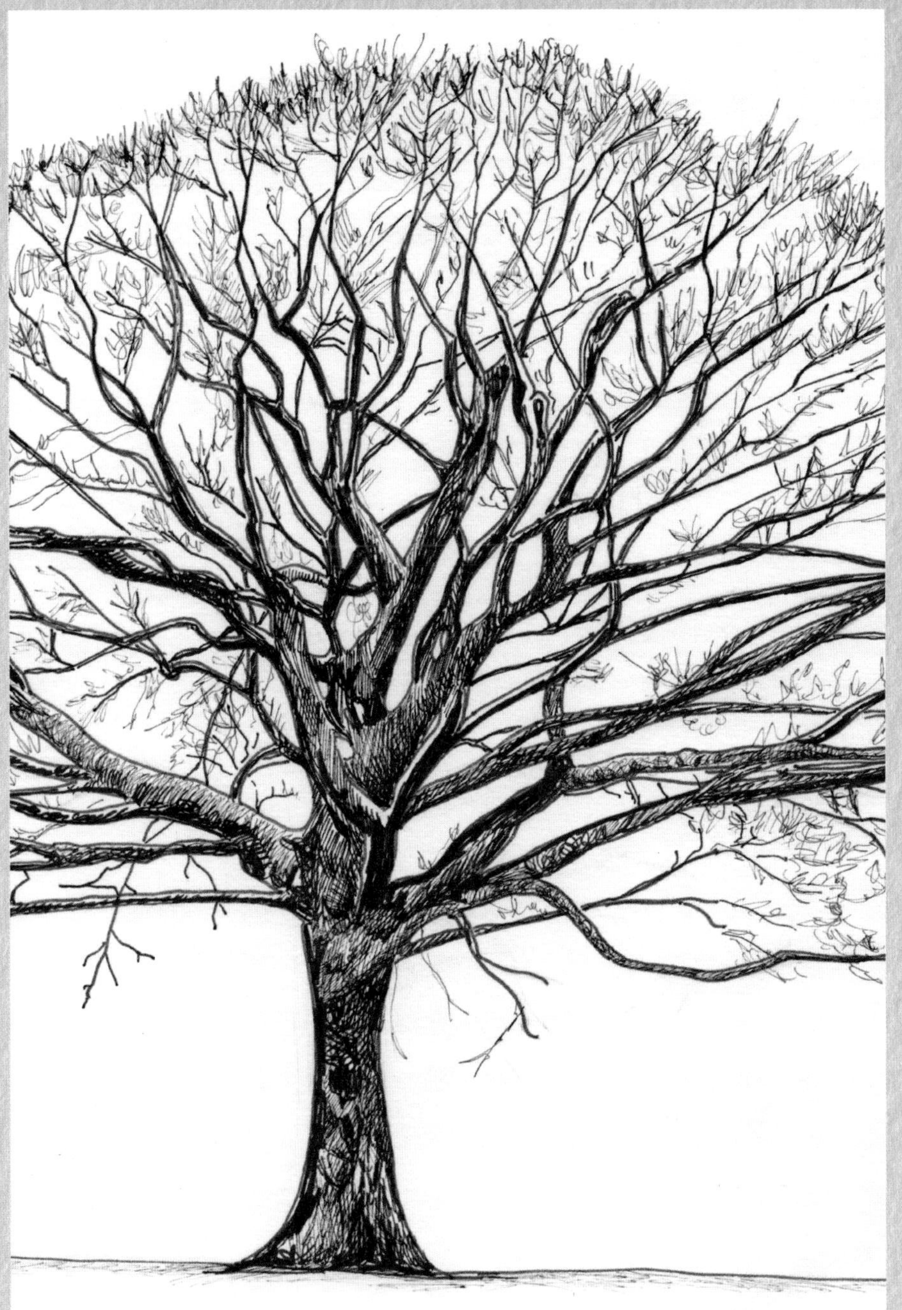

Lesson 5

Pine Cones

Following on from the simple structures of Chapter 1, we will look at a more complex structure in this lesson: a pine cone in graphite pencil. Pine cones have a fascinating natural history: female cones, the ones we are likely to find, are responsible for spreading the seeds, which are small, winged, and hidden inside the spiral of scales. The cones open and close with the weather – opening out with warmer, drier conditions and closing up in the cold and wet. This characteristic can be manipulated for sketching at different stages of this process.

For this complex structure, we will also develop graphite sketching a little further by using a wider tonal range of pencil softness – I suggest HB, 2B, 4B, and 6B. Use the harder pencils (HB and 2B) for outlines and details, and the softer pencils (4B and 6B) for shading. Remember to keep your pencils sharp.

Use a single photograph or select one angle of your real pine cone for this initial exercise. You can then experiment with different angles and perhaps even incorporate some colour in a more varied sketchbook page later on. If your chosen tree does not have cones, either find a cone for this exercise or choose a different, more complex structure from your tree to explore.

1 First, coax your pine cone to open slightly under warmer conditions. This will create a broad range of tones (a closed cone is unlikely to exhibit enough tonal variety). Ensure that there is a good light source, casting the interior of the cone into the shade. An adjustable desk lamp can work well, or position your cone close to a window, allowing in some natural light.

2 Using an HB pencil, begin with an initial outline to help position the drawing on the page and determine your preferred size. A larger than life-size drawing can be effective for complex structures, making it simpler to incorporate all the details. You might choose to add a few lateral lines around the cone to help decide where the main "layers" of scales will be positioned.

3 Working from top to bottom, fill in the scales with a 2B pencil, taking care to examine the angles of the scales in the more open portions. You might find it easier to first study the shape of each scale, as shown in the Gallery. Take your time during this stage, and press lightly with your pencil until you are more certain about your lines. Gradually fill out the rest of the cone. If you struggle with the complexity, make sure you break down the cone into "layers" first, indicating the areas of open and closed scales. Keep your pencil marks soft, so it is easy to erase any mistakes.

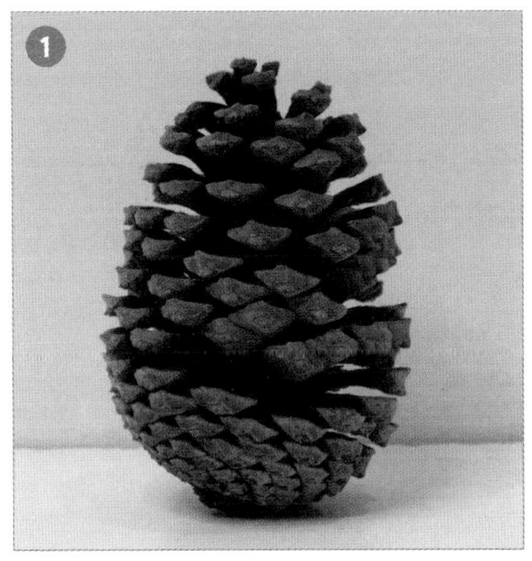

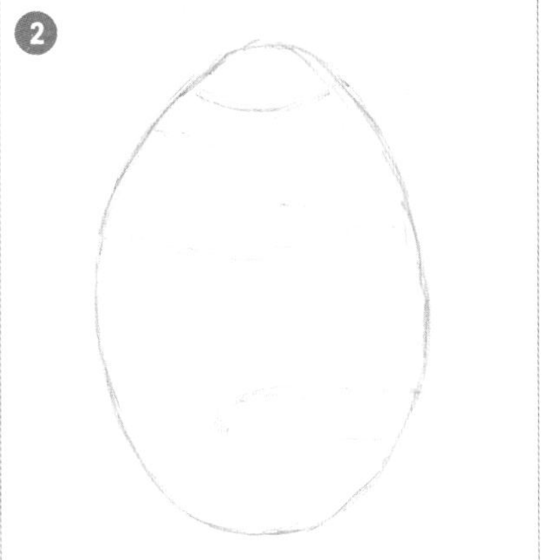

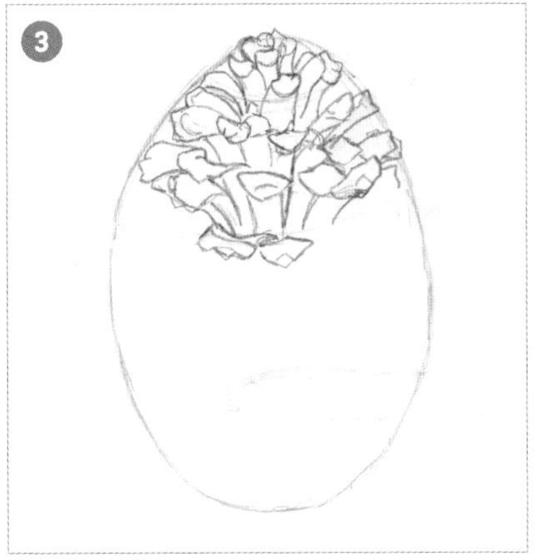

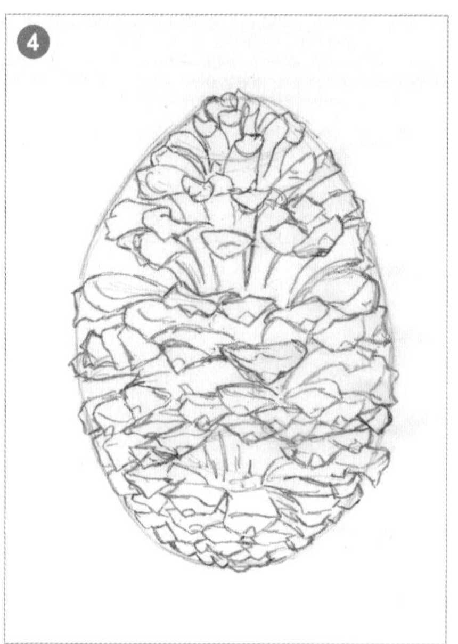

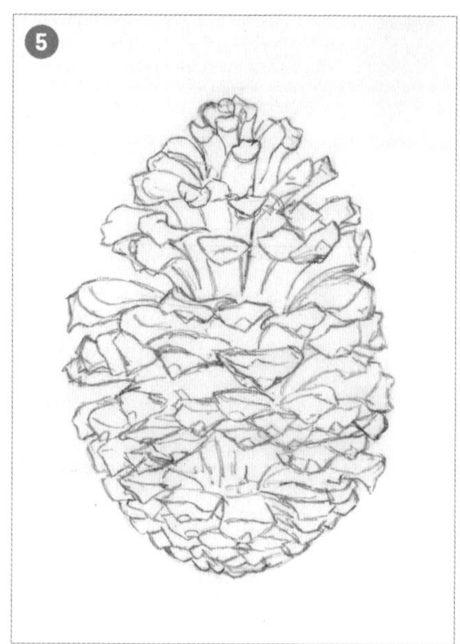

❹ When you are happy with the overall shape of each of the scale "layers", fill in the details of the tip of the scale and the angle of its descent into the central structure. It may help you keep track if you touch each scale with your finger as you draw it.

❺ Use a pointed or battery-operated eraser to carefully remove guide pencil lines from where they are no longer needed.

TIP:

Keep your pencils sharp as you work to ensure crisp lines and controlled shapes. Stop regularly to check the pencil's point and have your pencil sharpener close to hand.

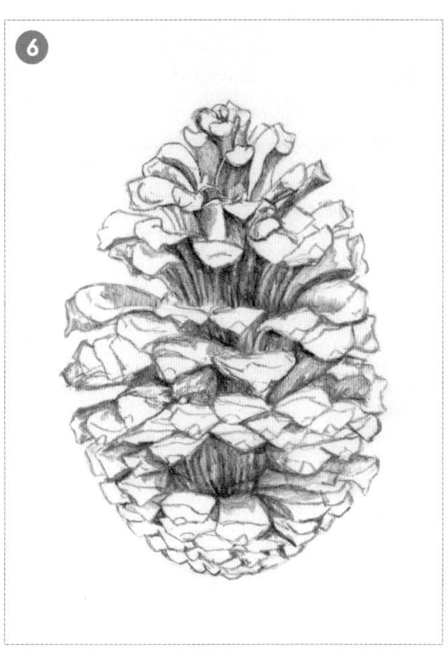

❻ Switch to the 6B pencil and fill in all the darkest areas of shadow. These are likely to be strongest where you can see deeper into the interior of the cone (where it has slightly opened out). Leave the shading on the outer scales for now.

❼ Finally, use your 4B pencil to fill in the intricate details of the outer scales. Some of these can be left very close to the colour of the paper. This will help to give the appearance of depth, with the closer and brighter scales receiving more detail but lighter shading than the densely shaded interior.

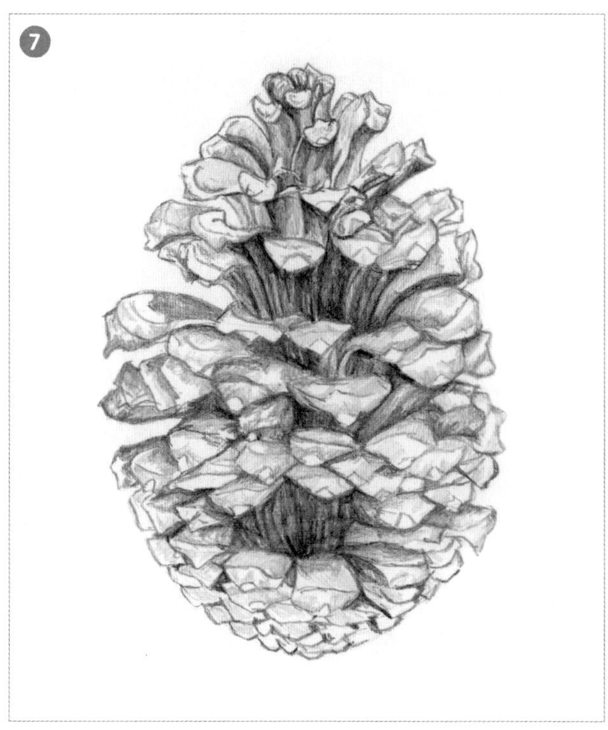

Gallery

Now try looking at the cone from a range of angles and fill your sketchbook page. These larch cones have a different shape and scale structure to the pine cones in the previous exercise. You could add a little coloured pencil to these sketchbook pages as embellishments, including a light layer directly after completing the initial sketch. Add your softer graphite drawing over the top of the coloured pencil for a subtle effect.

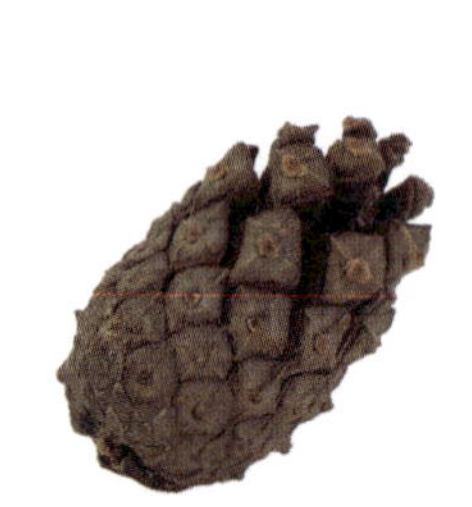

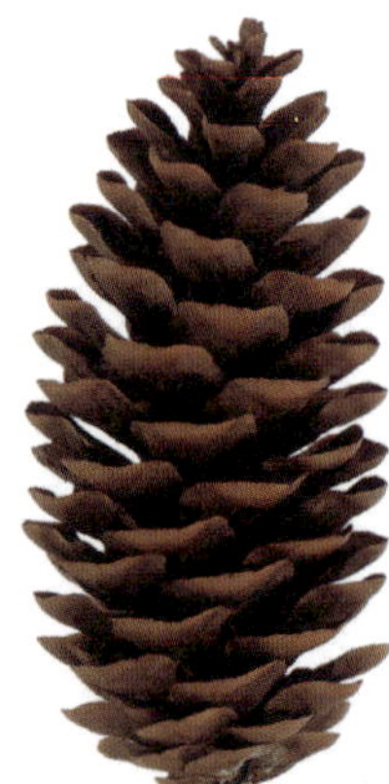

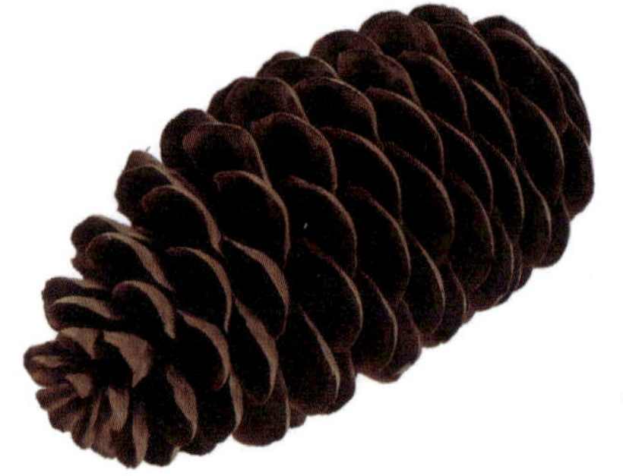

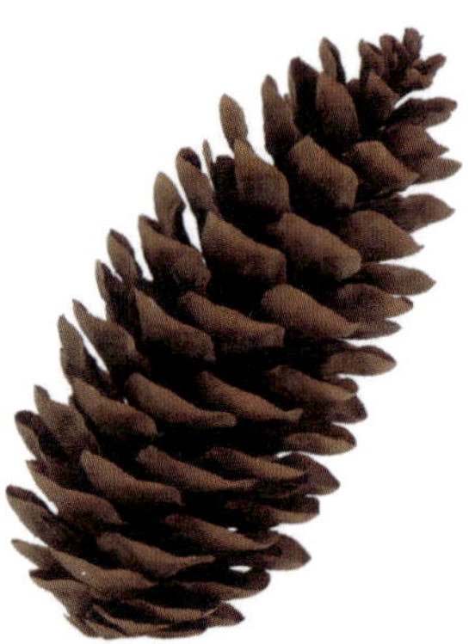

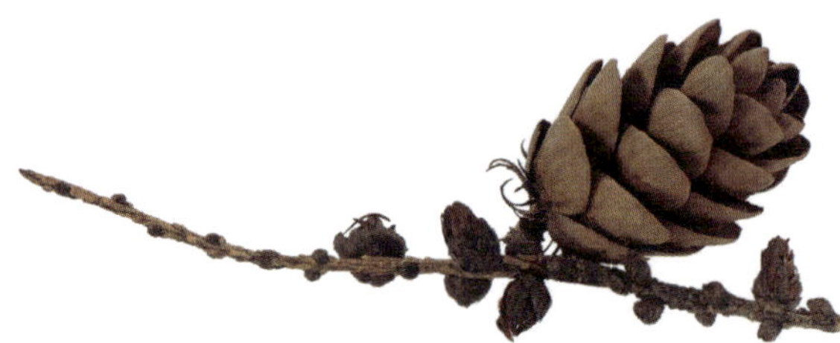

FIR AND LARCH CONES

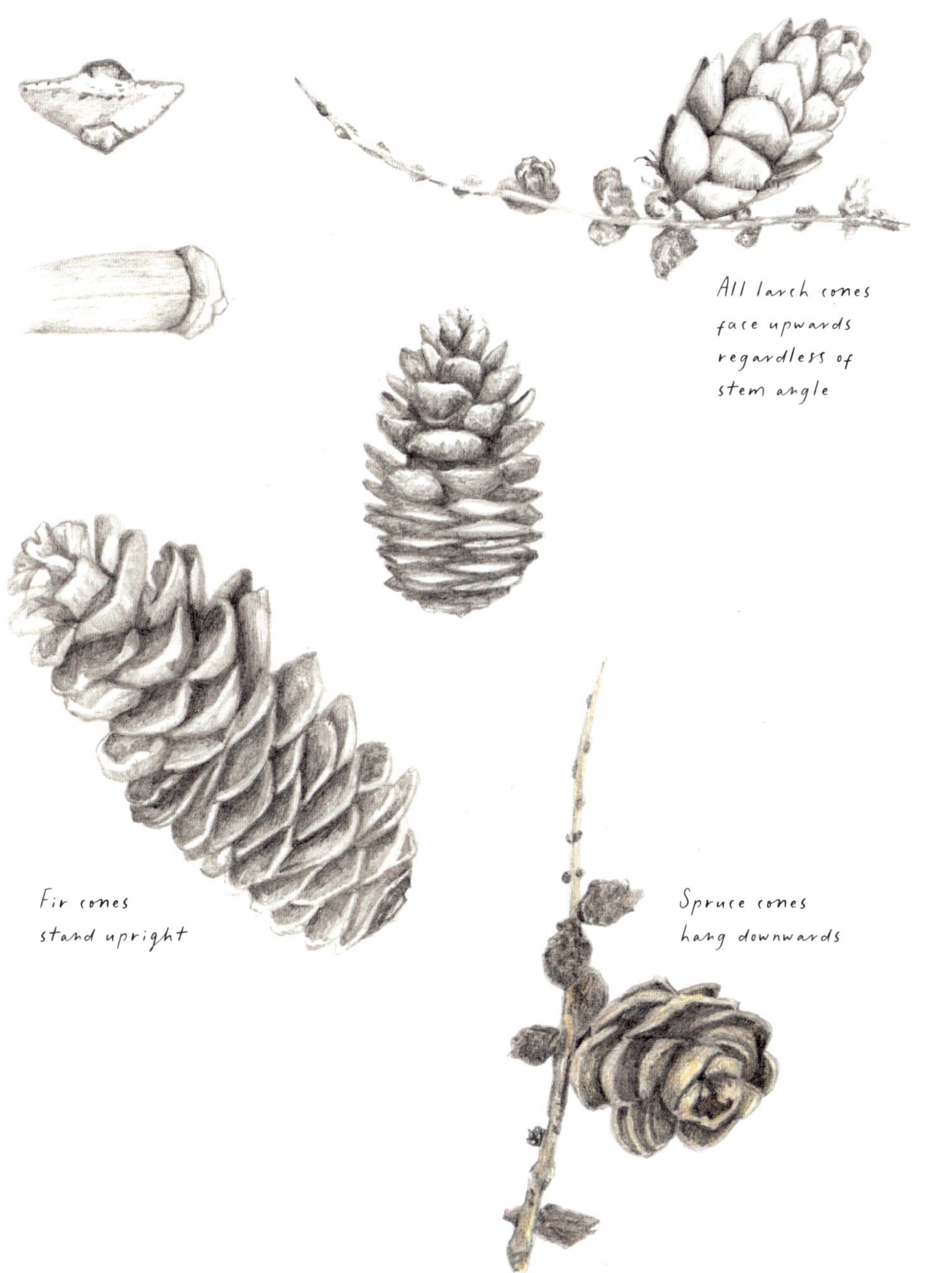

Lesson 6

Winter Tree

The shapes of deciduous trees in winter are fascinating for the artist, as you can really see the structure of the tree itself without the leaves getting in the way. As mentioned in Lesson 1, to really capture the character of an individual tree, it is necessary to understand its anatomy – the unique pattern of branches that give it its shape. Winter is the perfect time to really see what is going on under the foliage.

Continuing on the theme of complex structures, we will now expand the “stick tree” idea to more complicated winter tree shapes. Black fineliners are perfect for drawing the skeletal form of a bare tree; ensure you have some thin nibs, such as 0.1 or 0.05, to also add texture and interest to the tree branches.

This exercise is best done from a photograph of your tree as it is easy to lose track of all the branches outdoors, and you might get a little cold! Try not to be overwhelmed by the sheer complexity or density of branches – starting with the stick tree method, it is possible to simplify the shape and help you find your way around. Take this exercise steadily with regular breaks.

❶ Find a reference photo of your winter tree. This exercise is easiest if the tree is isolated from others with a bright sky behind it. If this is not possible, you will just need to take a little more care to ensure that the branches that you are drawing definitely originate from your chosen tree and not its neighbours.

❷ Begin with a graphite sketch in HB or 2B, to position your tree and ensure it will fit onto the page. Follow the advice in Lesson 1 to ensure that the trunk and canopy outline are positioned at a suitable size for your paper. Fill in the "stick tree" again, taking note of where the most prominent branches emerge from the trunk. This stage is important and may take a few tries. Keep your pencil lines light and use an eraser when needed.

❸ Still working in graphite, using a sharp, softer pencil such as 4B, add more details to your stick tree, fleshing out the branches to give them some bulk. Even though the intent is to make a fineliner drawing, the majority of the hard work will be done in graphite. The direction of your more detailed work will depend on whether you are right- or left-handed. As I am right-handed, I worked from left to right, thus avoiding smudging.

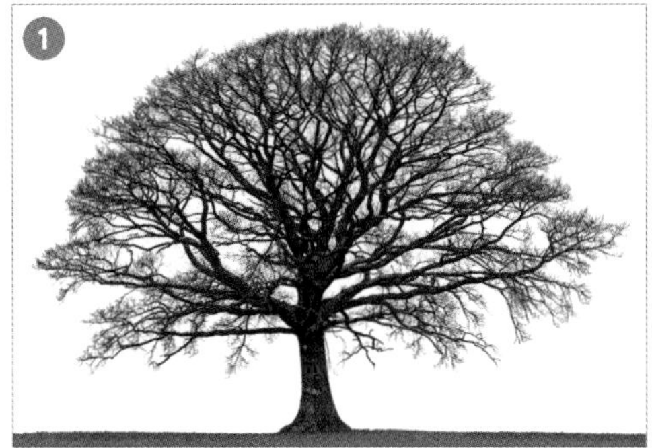

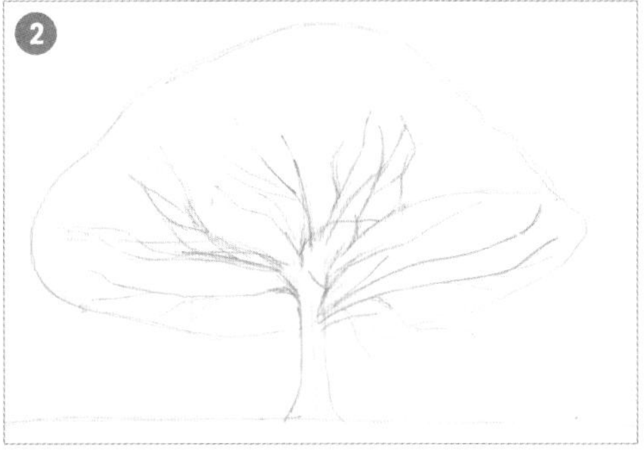

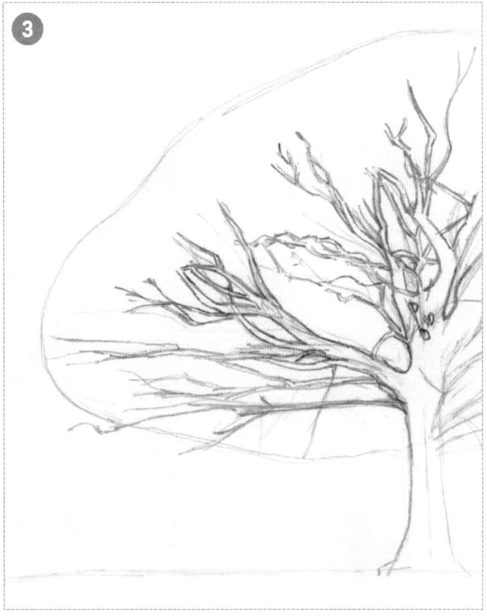

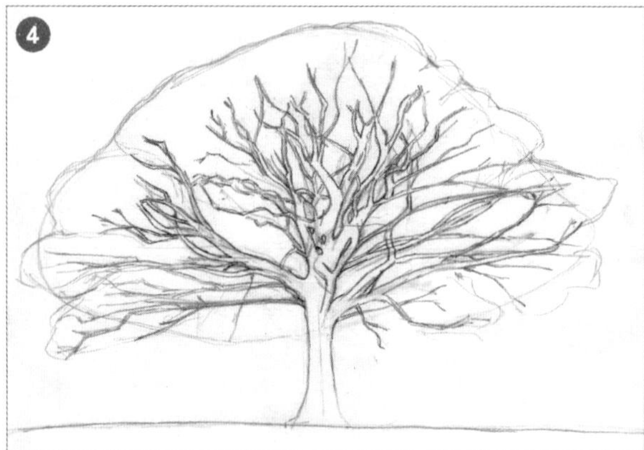

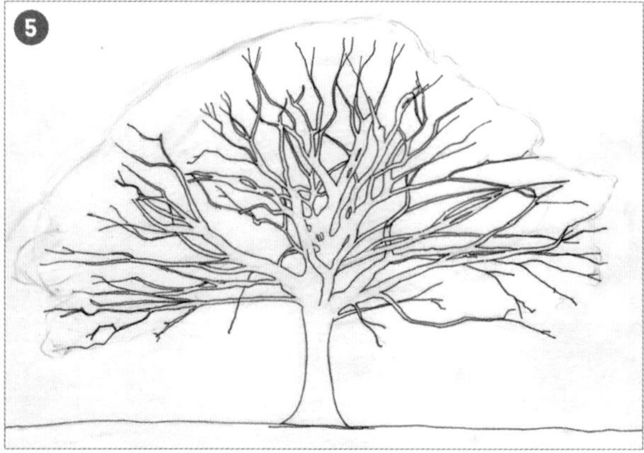

TIP:

If you lack very thin fineliners, you could make the overall drawing larger to avoid the lines coming out too thick for the intricate tree branches.

❹ Fill in the rest of the branch details in the same way – allow plenty of time and take breaks if you feel tired. It is better to do complex drawing tasks such as these branches with a rested mind. When you have filled out the full tree, draw around the top of the canopy again, marking the extent of the finest branches.

❺ Gather your fineliners. You will need one thicker size for the main trunk and diminishing sizes for the branches; I used 0.3, 0.2, 0.1, and 0.05. Begin with the thickest size and outline the trunk and any of the thickest main branches. Allow these branches to narrow to a single line of the same thickness as they reach away from the main trunk. Remove the pencil lines below, except for the canopy shape.

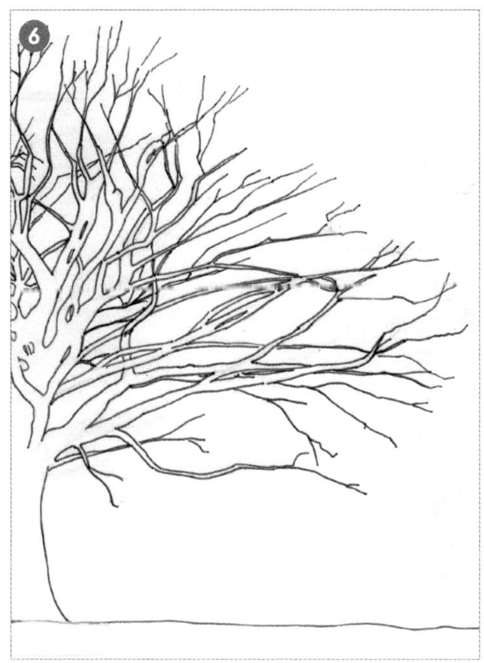

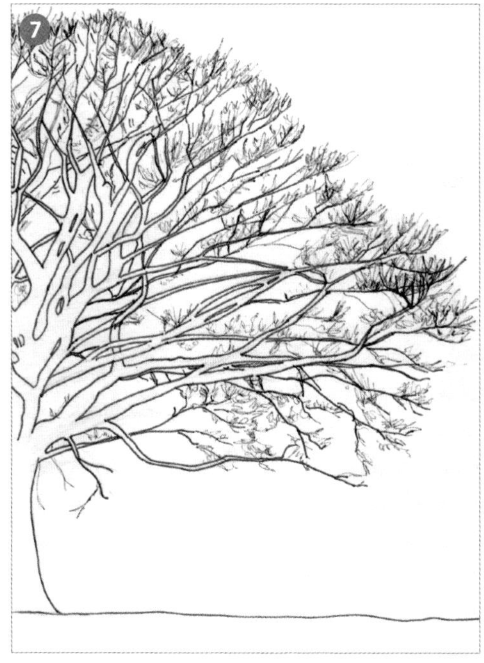

6 Using a thinner-tipped fineliner, continue each of these branches towards the canopy top. Look carefully at the structure of your tree – some finer branches may also appear from behind the boughs you have already drawn. Gradually allow the thinner lines to reach your delineated canopy top.

7 Fill in the finer twigs with relaxed, scratchy marks at the top of the canopy (and wherever else there are clear "tufts" of finer twigs). In my tree, the majority of these marks are at the top of the canopy and I drew them in freely with my 0.1 and 0.05 fineliners until the shape of the tree had been filled out.

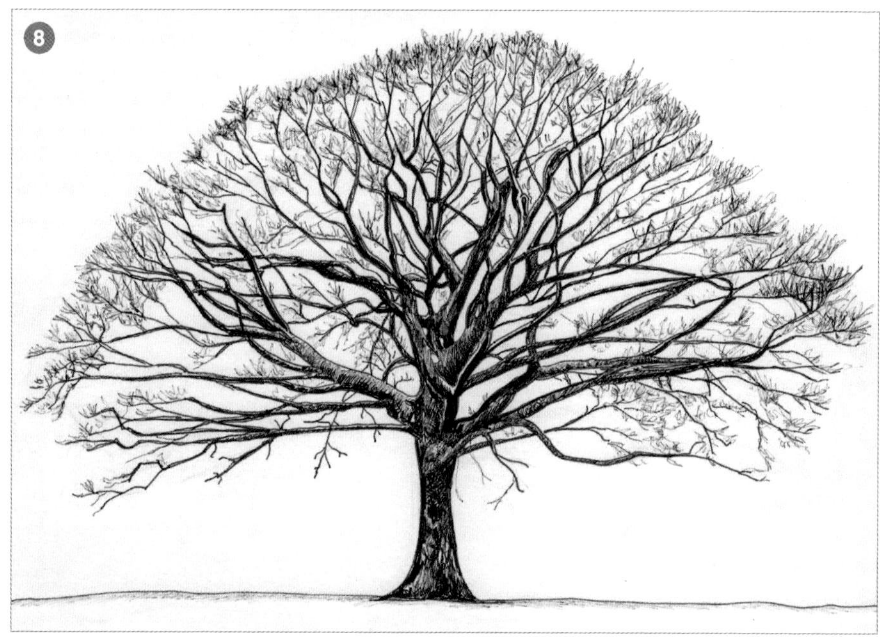

8 Finally, continuing to use your thinnest pens, add some shading to the trunk and main branches to give the tree some depth and shape. Move your pen in the direction of the shape of the trunk, to help the eye read the three-dimensionality of the trunk and branches, using hatching and cross-hatching to lighten or darken the tones.

Gallery

There is great variation in the structure of trees to be explored. Try focusing in on specific areas, such as the intricate branching of the trunk of this urban tree (right). Alternatively, you could reduce the level of detail and produce a winter silhouette. A black ink brush pen was used to darken the trunk of the roadside example (below).

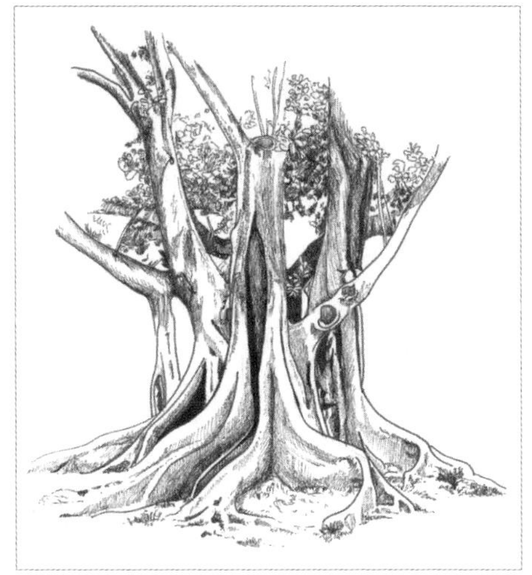

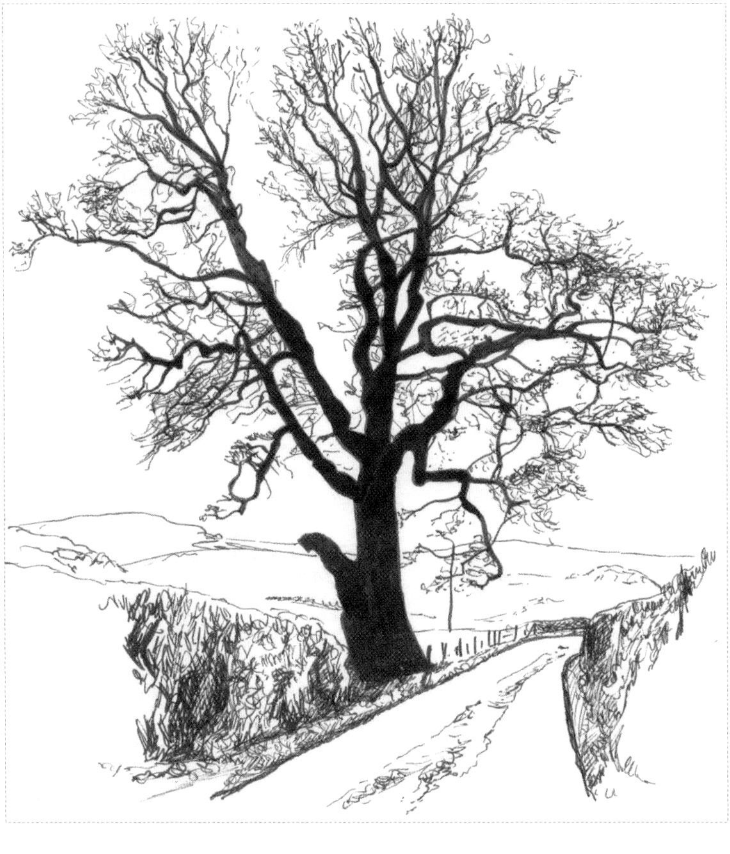

Lesson 7

Blossom in Colour

There is little more uplifting than the sight of a fruit tree in blossom. Drawing tree flowers can be challenging, in terms of both the intricacies of the flowers and achieving an aesthetically pleasing background. Typically, we think of fruit trees when considering blossoms: cherries, apples, and the exotic flowers of some tropical fruits. However, many trees will have some form of flower if you know what to look for.

Bear in mind that some trees have a specific sex: your tree might be male (producing pollen), female (producing fruit and seeds), or a mixture on different branches. Finding out the sex of your tree can be fascinating – try nature journaling your tree and don't be surprised if it varies in its reproductive structures over the years.

Building from the coloured pencil techniques used for the fruit in Lesson 3, we can now try a more complex floral structure with a soft background. I am using the glorious blossoms of domestic fruit trees to demonstrate, but a similar approach can be used for whatever flowers you find. The pencil-sharpenings technique described here may also be useful to create backgrounds for studies of other tree parts, such as leaves.

Additional materials:

Stubby paintbrush, burnisher pencil

❶ Use a flower photograph with a relatively simple background. I have selected a branch of cherry blossom against a bright blue sky. Set out your coloured pencils, selecting colours that match as closely as possible to those in the photograph. Swatching colours can be useful to help you match and blend.

❷ Begin with a graphite sketch to position your flower on the page. If you wish, use a fineliner to give your drawing a neat outline and erase the graphite lines. Here, I used a graphite-coloured fineliner to give a soft but clear edge. If your blossoms are pale, ensure that the graphite lines have been drawn softly or "knocked back" with an eraser before commencing colouring.

❸ To create a soft background, sharpen a coloured pencil of your chosen colour onto the paper. You could blend this with more than one colour if you wish. Remove as many of the wood shavings as possible by hand. Now, with a stubby paintbrush, use a firm circular motion to rub the sharpenings into the paper, creating a subtle background. This may take several layers.

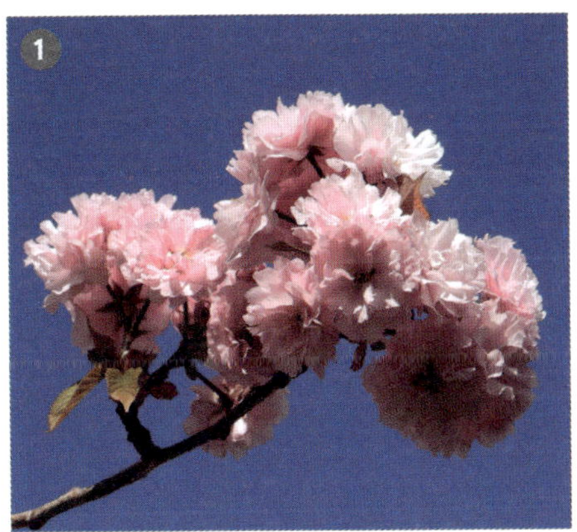

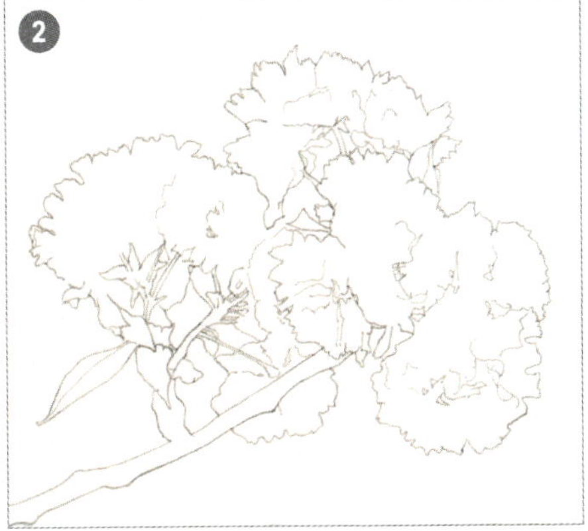

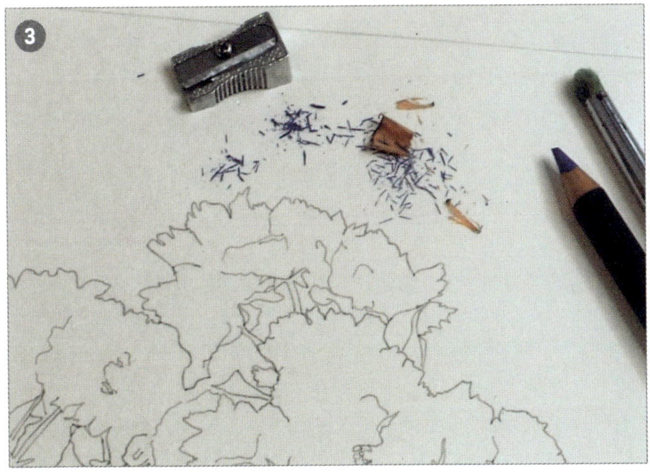

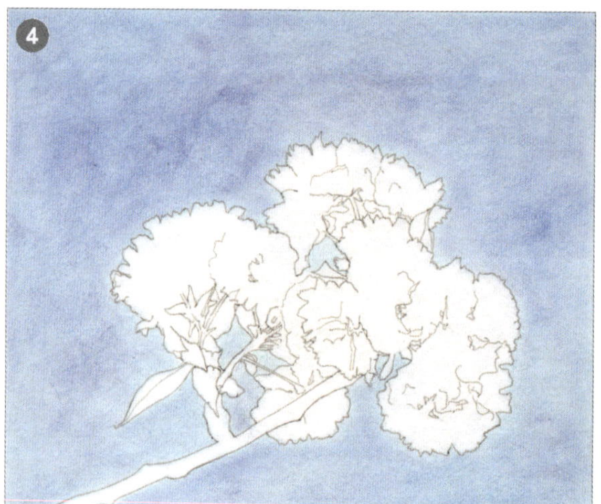

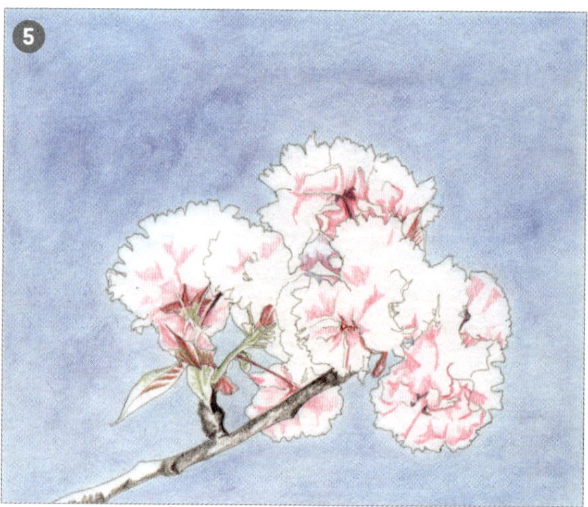

TIP:

Place spare paper under your hand once the background is done. This will help avoid smudging and loss of colour through transfer onto your skin.

❹ Use a sharp pencil that is the same colour as the background to tidy the edges around the line drawing. Use a pointed or battery-operated eraser to remove any colour straying into the drawing.

❺ Now find the shadows in among the flower petals. Use a sharp pencil to colour these in, finding all areas of the same colour throughout the entire image to save time. Finding the darkest areas and adding these first can help you to check that the composition is balanced.

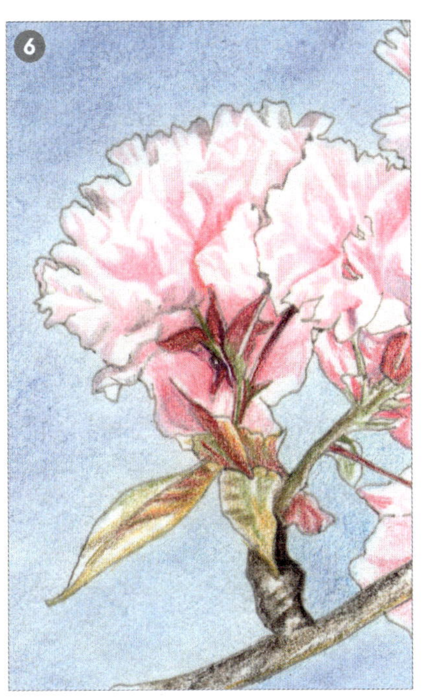

❻ If you are happy with the balance of darks and lights, start to blend the edges into the centre of the petal. Look for the folds of the petals and other textures that help to give the flower its form. Use a sharp coloured pencil to carefully delineate these small shadows. Also add details of any leaves and twigs at this time.

❼ Continue to build up the layers, making sure that you leave some areas to catch the light and provide contrast to the shadows. You may need to add a few areas of dense colour at this stage. Keep a critical eye on your reference photo and try to ensure a good balance of light and shade. As you did in Lesson 3, give your drawing a final layer of "burnisher" pencil, or a light colour from your set, to blend the colours together and remove any areas of paper showing through.

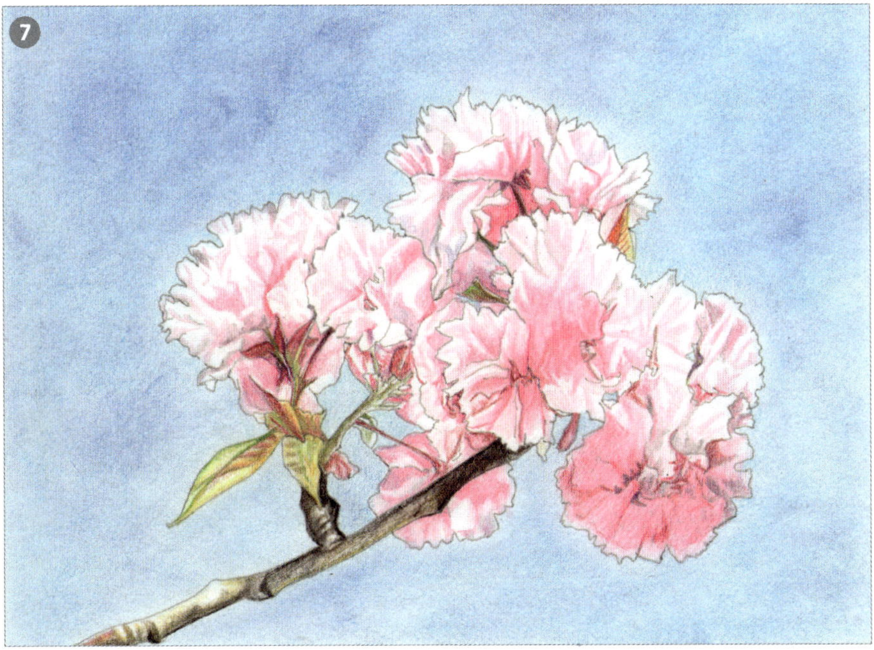

Gallery

As a next step, try adding the flowers in the context of a more complex background. For this apple tree, laden with blossoms, I heavily edited the number of branches from the reference photo in order to create a good balance between subject and sky. Here, instead of the pencil-sharpenings method, the sky was laid on strongly by hand, giving the image a bolder aesthetic.

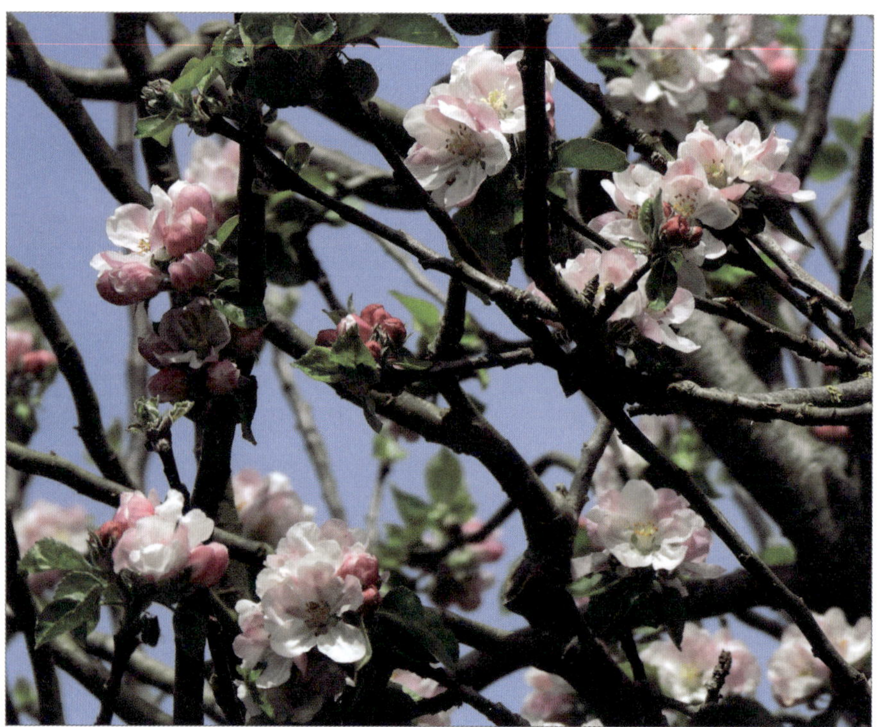

TIP:

When covering large areas in a single background colour, you can press a little harder with your pencil than you would when blending two or more colours. You will eventually want to "saturate" the background in the colour of that single pencil. If you need to blend across these large areas, practise being consistent with the amount of pressure and the order in which the colours are being laid down to avoid one patch of colour looking different from another. Burnishing is likely to be important in this case to make the blend of the two colours more seamless and uniform. This is where practising your swatching and blending will reveal its benefit – it is always best to give a technique a try first on a scrap piece of the same paper as your final composition, rather than risk patchy and uneven results.

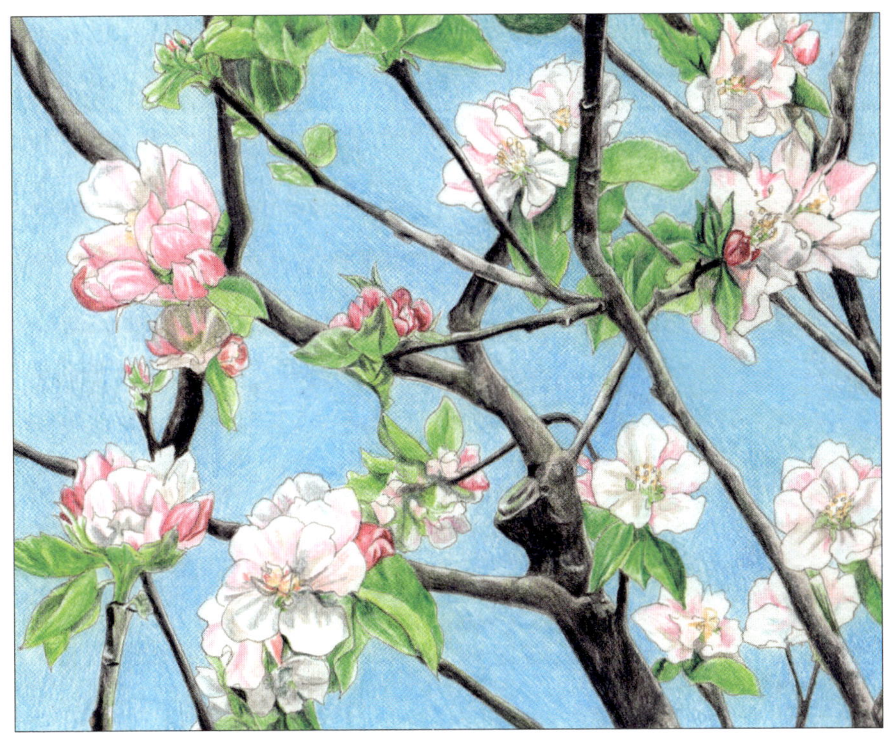

Lesson 8

Tree Grid

As you practise observing your tree through the year, you will notice more and more of the interesting structures that we have considered in this chapter. As well as directly recording your observations, there are many ways you can celebrate your tree and share your knowledge. In this exercise, you will use your explorations to make a beautiful grid of sketches, using all the different artistic media you have studied so far.

In the previous lessons, you have looked at the overall shape of the tree, its fruits, flowers, seeds, and winter form. Now, we are going to combine different aspects of the tree into a single sheet, which can be used as a reference guide to help you identify the tree in future, or as a place to practise a variety of artistic methods side by side and make comparisons.

This grid exercise is full of possibilities. You might choose to focus on just the one tree and examine selected parts or angles in each box in a different medium each time. Or, you might consider the variation found between your tree and other local species but using the same artistic style. The steps below are just suggestions, so have fun with the creation of a tree grid for your unique artistic interests.

Additional materials:

Ruler, scissors

1 Gather a selection of photographs or samples from your tree. You may need to build this resource over time, perhaps using your nature journal (see Lesson 4) as a guide and mine of information.

2 Split your page into a grid using a pencil and ruler. The number of columns and rows will depend on the size of your paper and the intended number of subjects or artistic methods. For my A4 (letter size) sheet, I split the paper into a 4 x 4 grid (four rows and four columns).

3 Now decide on how you will use your boxes. I chose four trees and made a chart to highlight the differences between them. I assigned a tree to each column and then sketched the nuts or seeds in the top row, the leaf shape in the second row, the flowers in the third row, and the appearance of the winter twigs in the bottom row.

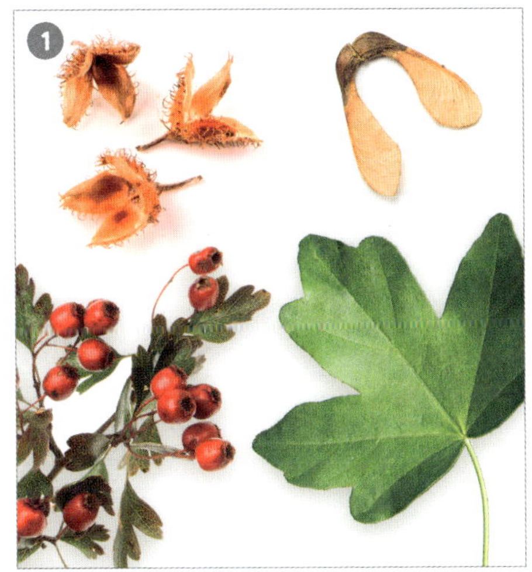

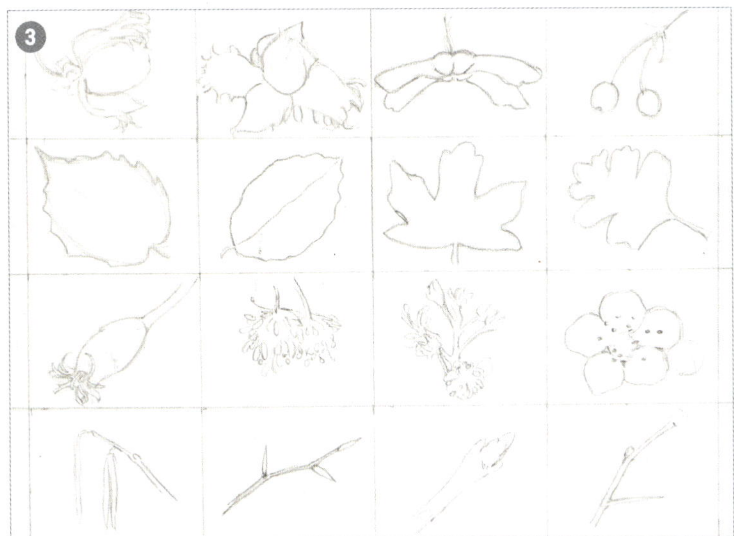

❹ Remove the grid pencil lines using a pointed or battery-operated eraser or, alternatively, make a feature of them by drawing them in with a fineliner and a ruler. Add some colour or detail. In this example, I chose not to use fineliner and instead added coloured pencil over the top of the soft graphite outline. Using the same style for every box brings the focus onto the different choices of tree subject. You could also add some written notes to support your drawings.

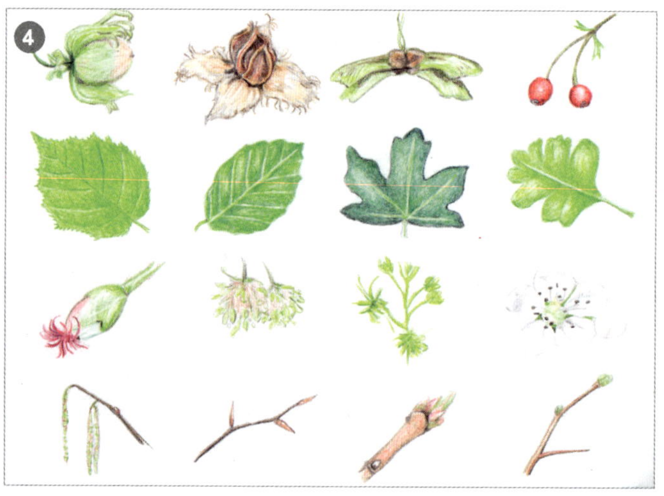

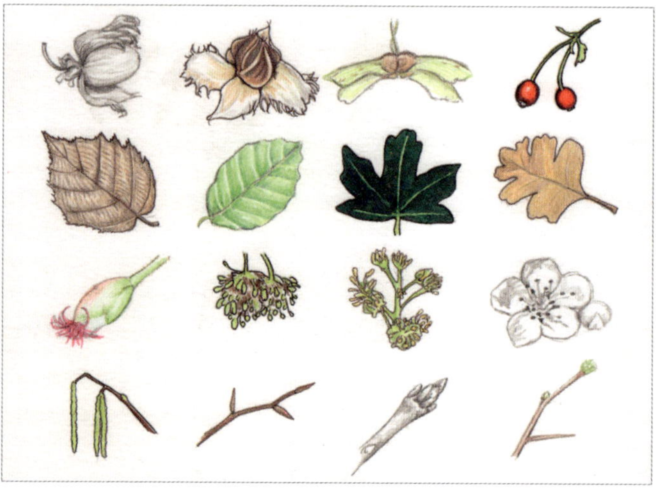

Another option is to use different artistic media throughout the grid. In this example, I mixed graphite drawings, fineliner, coloured pencil, and ink brush pens to give a varied effect and add visual interest.

Get Creative

One of the great things about these varied pages of sketches is their versatility for other uses. Why not try creating tree-themed bookmarks, greetings cards, or identification sheets using your tree grids?

These bookmarks were made by slicing through the columns of my finished tree grid with a pair of scissors. If preferred, you could draw around a favourite bookmark to get the size and then split this into boxes for your tree drawings.

To make informative and personal handmade tree greetings cards, fold a piece of card in half before beginning your grid. Make sure you have an envelope to fit!

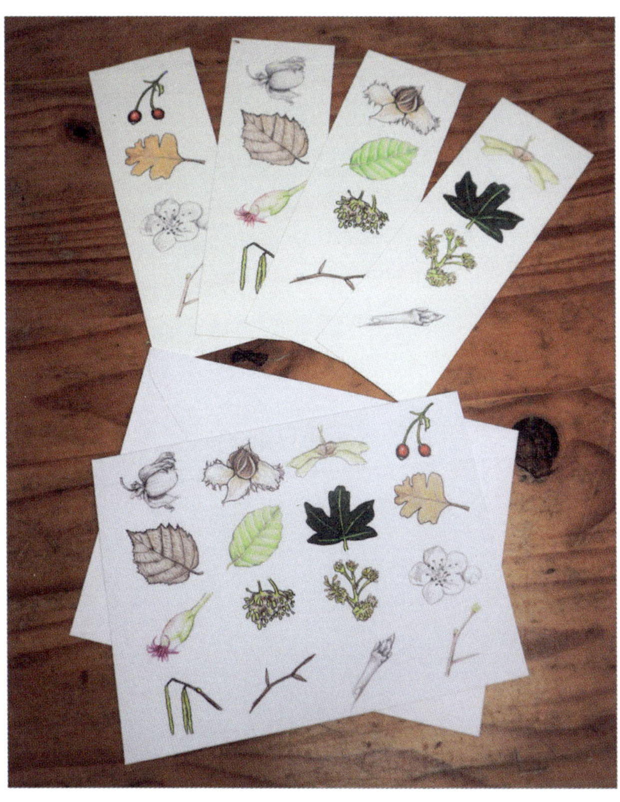

Making a Field Guide

Laminated field sheets are invaluable when looking at trees outdoors, and a hand-drawn example would make a wonderful gift. Use all the information you have gathered about your tree, together with the tree grid, to make an interesting sheet. Handwritten is all the more personal. Make sure you are happy with all your sketches and words before taking the final step and laminating. Your guide can be used alongside expert versions to help you internalise the information using examples from your own patch. See also Identifying Species.

Hazel *Corylus avellana*	**European beech** *Fagus sylvatica*
Edible nuts, outer green husk surrounds smooth shell. 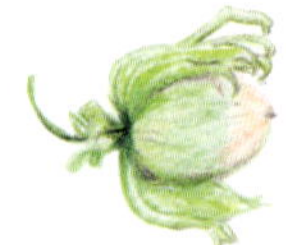	Beech nuts also known as mast. Triangular, edible when cooked but bitter, traditionally used to fatten pigs. 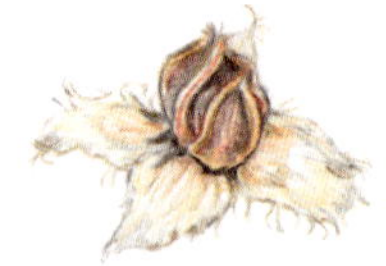
Leaves are round to oval but pointed at tip, doubly toothed, downy soft to touch. 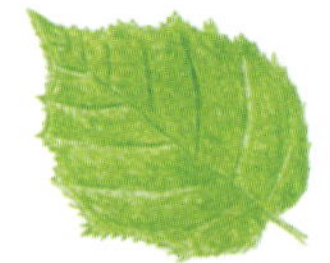	Young leaves are lime green with hairs, which they lose later. Oval and pointed at tip. Beautiful autumn colours. 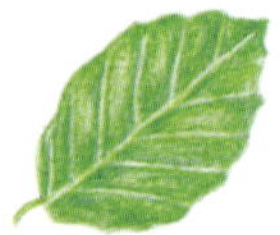
Female flowers in late winter to early spring. Emerges from bud. 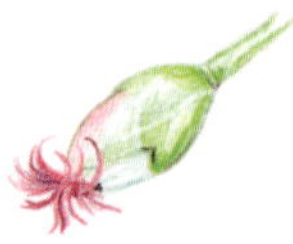	Flowers are hanging tassels, male flower shown here. 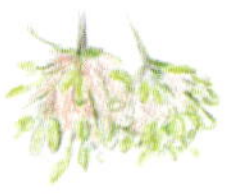
Rounded buds with male catkin emerging in early spring. Extending to release yellow pollen. 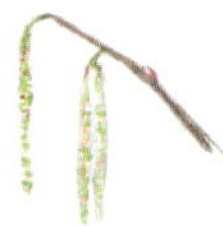	Pointed buds make this tree easy to spot in winter. 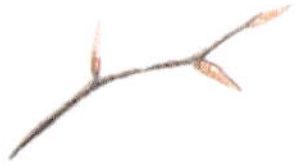

Field maple ***Acer campestre***	**Common hawthorn** ***Crataegus monogyna***
Winged seeds common to maples.	Stalked red berries known as "haws", edible and used in jellies.
Leaves are five-lobed with rounded teeth.	Leaves are small with toothed lobes and turn a bright yellow in autumn.
Flowers contain both male and female parts and hang in groups.	Prolific white flowers in May, flat clusters of blooms along the top of branches.
Winter buds grow in opposite pairs.	Sharp thorns on twigs with round, red, protruding buds in winter.

Don't confuse hawthorn with blackthorn, *Prunus spinosa*, which flowers before leaf emergence. Hawthorn comes into leaf first and flowers later.

Chapter 3

Trees in the Landscape

So far, we have looked at the whole tree in isolation and focused in on interesting parts such as flowers, leaves, and fruit. In this chapter, we will look at the tree in company: woodlands, forests, and trees in the wider landscape. You will learn to edit a busy scene and discover creative ways to convey the presence of trees among the abundance of vegetation that surrounds them.

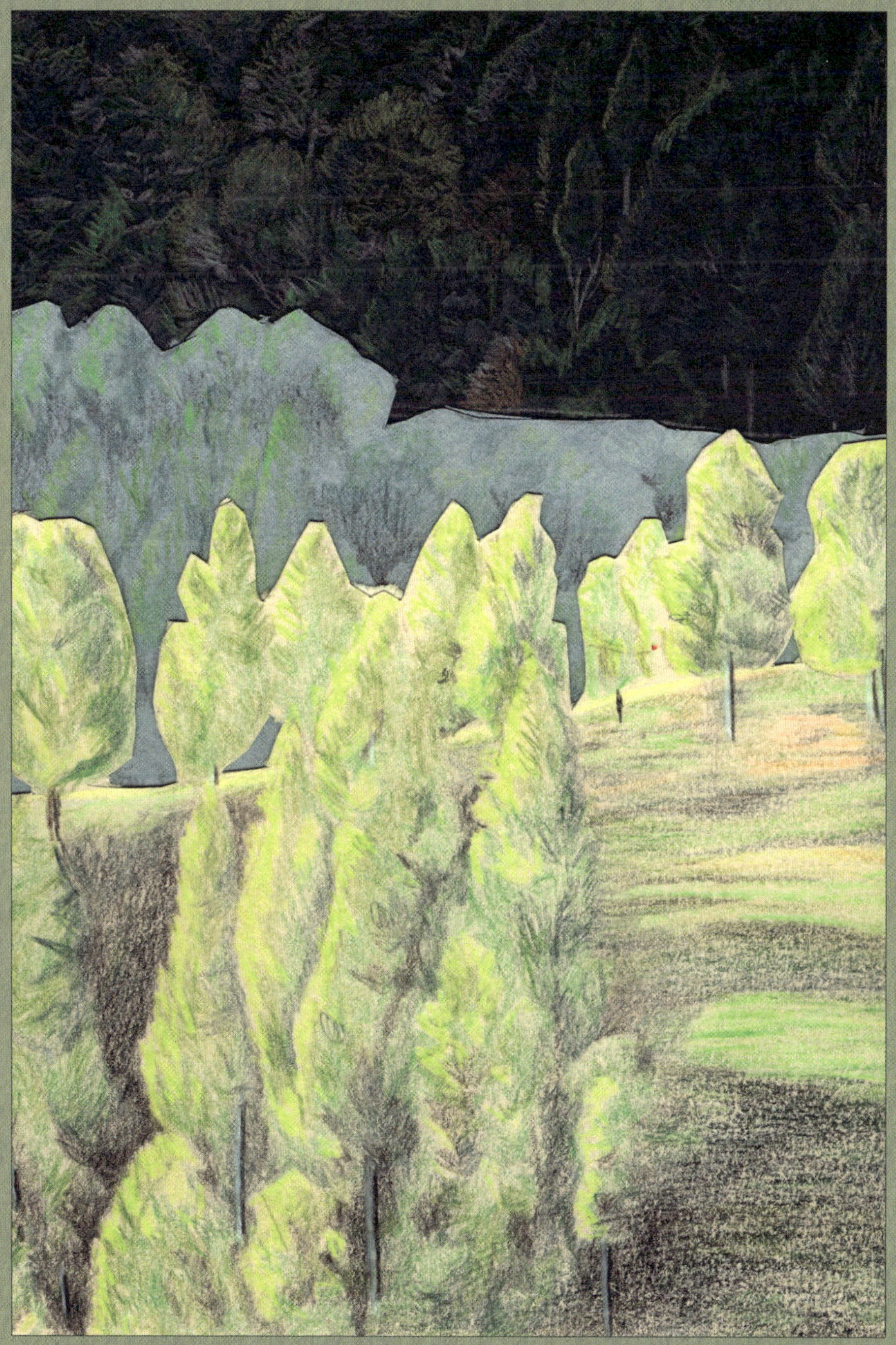

Lesson 9

Verdant Forest

To begin exploring the topic of trees in the wider landscape, there is no better example (or artistic challenge) than the tropical rainforest, where trees crowd together with a great variety of other verdant plants in competition for light and water.

Tackling the dense vegetation of the woodland scene in graphite is an interesting challenge. Using this Amazonian example, I will show you how to set your tree centre stage in a complex scene. You will learn that it is possible to achieve a good effect of vegetation without the necessity to draw every leaf and branch.

For this exercise, it will be particularly important to keep your pencils sharp and have a pointed or battery-operated eraser to hand. Ensure that you have a good range of pencil hardnesses ready (H–6B), along with a reference photo of your tree surrounded by the greenery of others.

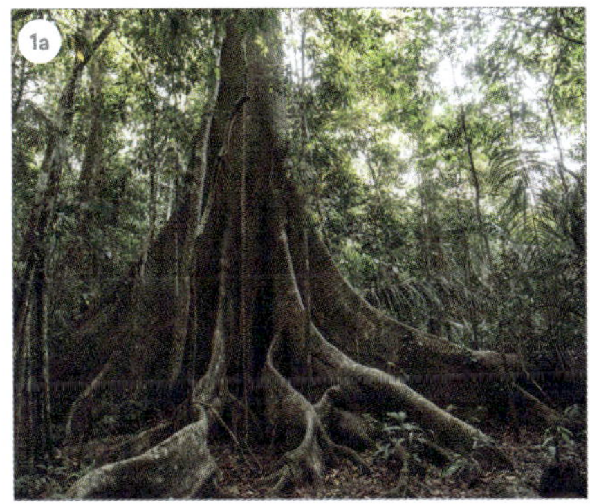

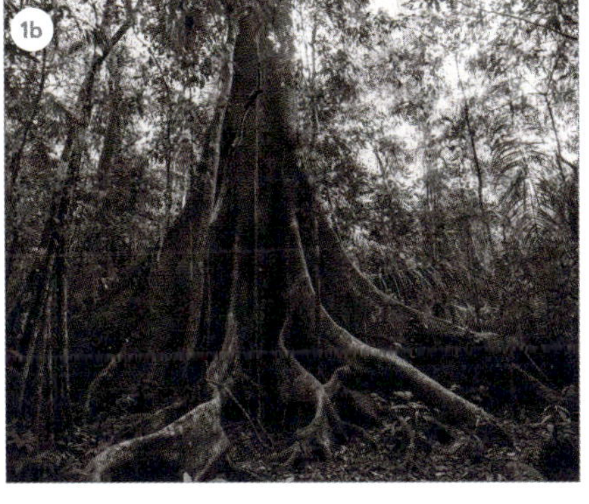

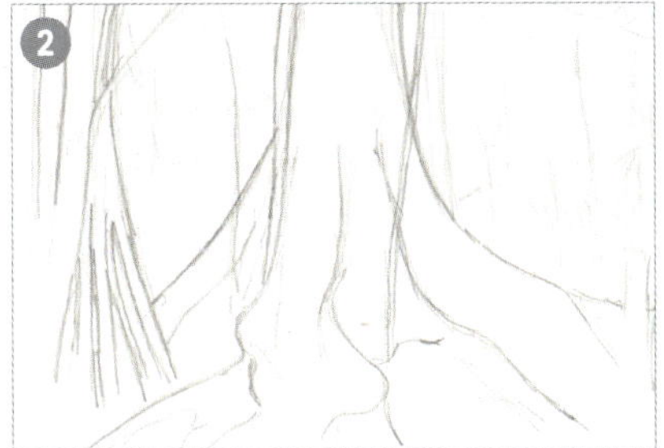

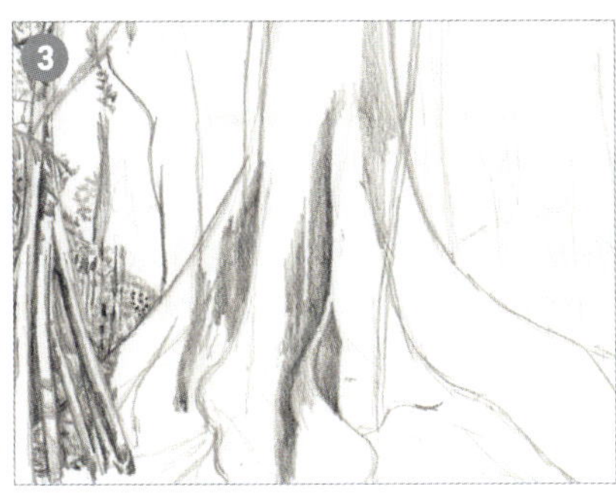

1 Begin with a reference photo of your chosen tree in a woodland or forest setting (1a). To make judging tonal values easier, convert your photo into greyscale (1b), by either using a filter or printing it out in black and white. Experiment with your filter; a cooler or warmer version of greyscale can help enhance the values.

2 Using HB or 2B, make a graphite sketch to position the main elements of the scene. Here, I focused on the large lupuna tree. You may wish to crop your photo to centre your tree and, when sketching, remove branches or other background items that interfere with the composition. Sketch out all the main features, such as the position of the trunk and main branches, and the structural elements of the surrounding trees.

3 Beginning in the top left (if you are right-handed) or top right (if you are left-handed), start to build detail. Think of your previous stage as a map to which you are now adding all the detailed information. Use a harder pencil (H, HB, or 2B) for the furthest leaves, adding them as squiggly marks. Try to retain an indication of leaf shape in these marks.

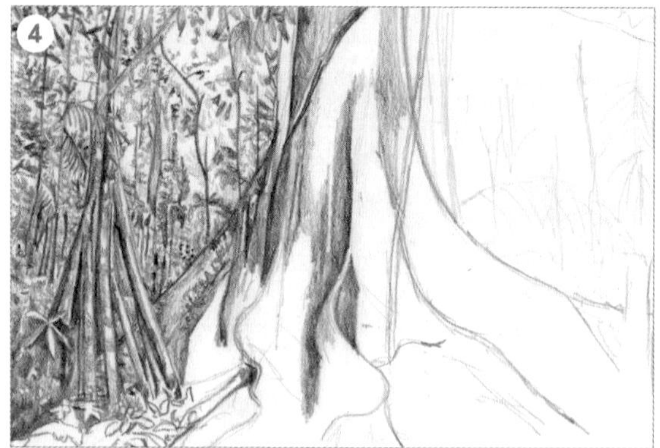

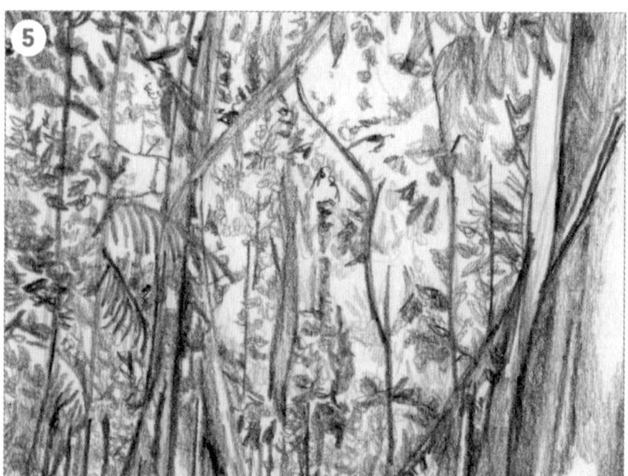

TIP:

Use a spare sheet of paper underneath your hand to help avoid smudging as you work into the picture. Glassine or tracing paper is best for this purpose.

❹ Use the softer pencils (4B and 6B, sharpened) for areas of shadow, identified from your greyscale reference. These might be the undersides of branches or areas of leaves clustered together. Some of these may need to be laid over the top of your earlier leaf marks. Leave lighter areas as the colour of the paper.

❺ Look at the background leaves and identify some of the main shapes. Try to replicate these as you fill in the leaves in the background, ensuring some variety in light and dark. Continue to switch between hard and soft pencils. Keep marks light and playful, getting "the idea" of hundreds of leaves, without drawing them all. Look at the shapes made when leaves cluster together and leave some spaces white, the negative space, to allow light to shine through.

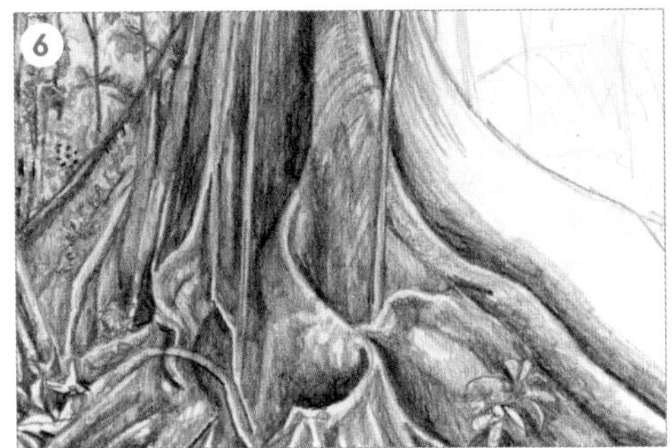

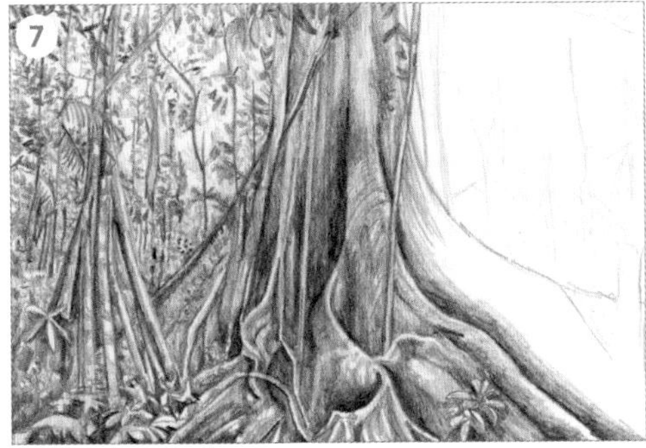

❻ Identify areas of shadow to emphasise on the trunk and main branches, using stronger tones for your focal tree to make it stand out. My lupuna has deep folds in the trunk and roots, which I rendered in strong 6B pencil, but I also added some lighter areas with emerging plants. Search out these little details to add interest.

❼ Continue to work across your drawing. If possible, try to avoid going back to areas, instead giving each region its due attention as you work, changing pencil as often as necessary.

❽ When you reach the edge, take a look at the overall balance of the drawing compared with your reference photo. It might be necessary to use a pointed or battery-operated eraser to bring a few areas back to the colour of the paper, adding highlights, or to darken some places with a sweep of strong 6B.

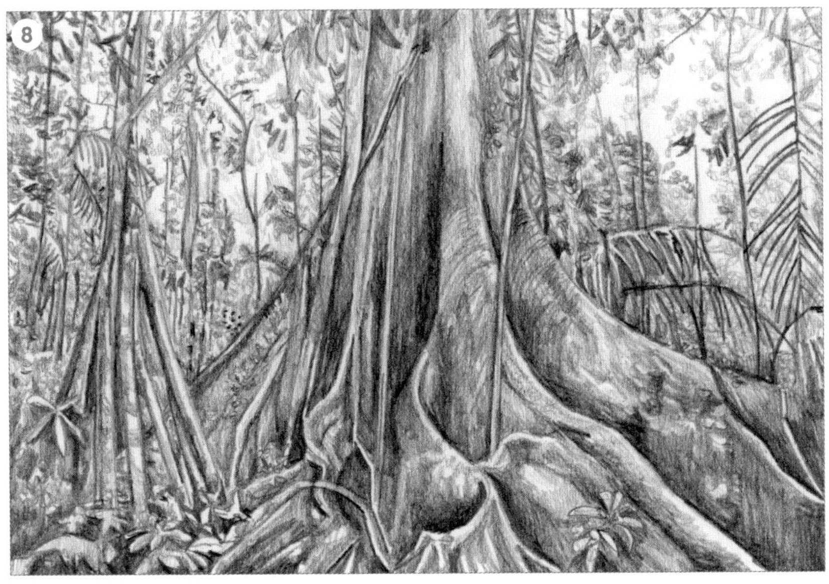

Gallery

In this temperate woodland scene, the majority of the leaves are located low down and the forest floor is cluttered with plants and fallen logs. After the initial sketch stage, I identified a few areas to highlight in colour to add interest to the graphite drawing. The snatches of coloured pencil were added just after the initial sketch had been done. The detailed graphite drawing was then layered over the top, allowing areas of colour to show through.

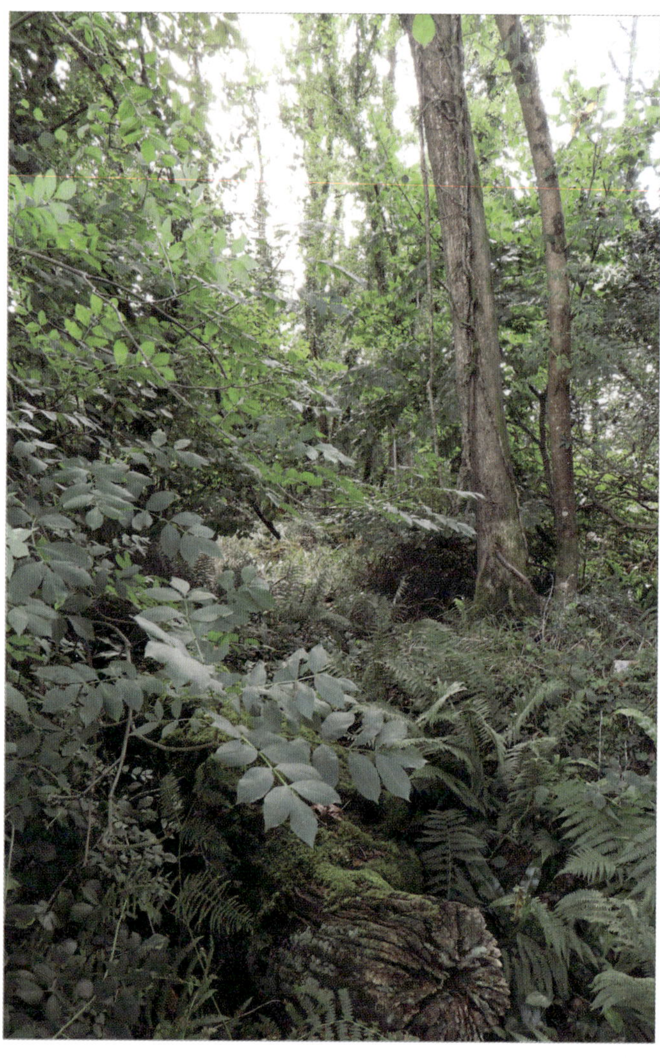

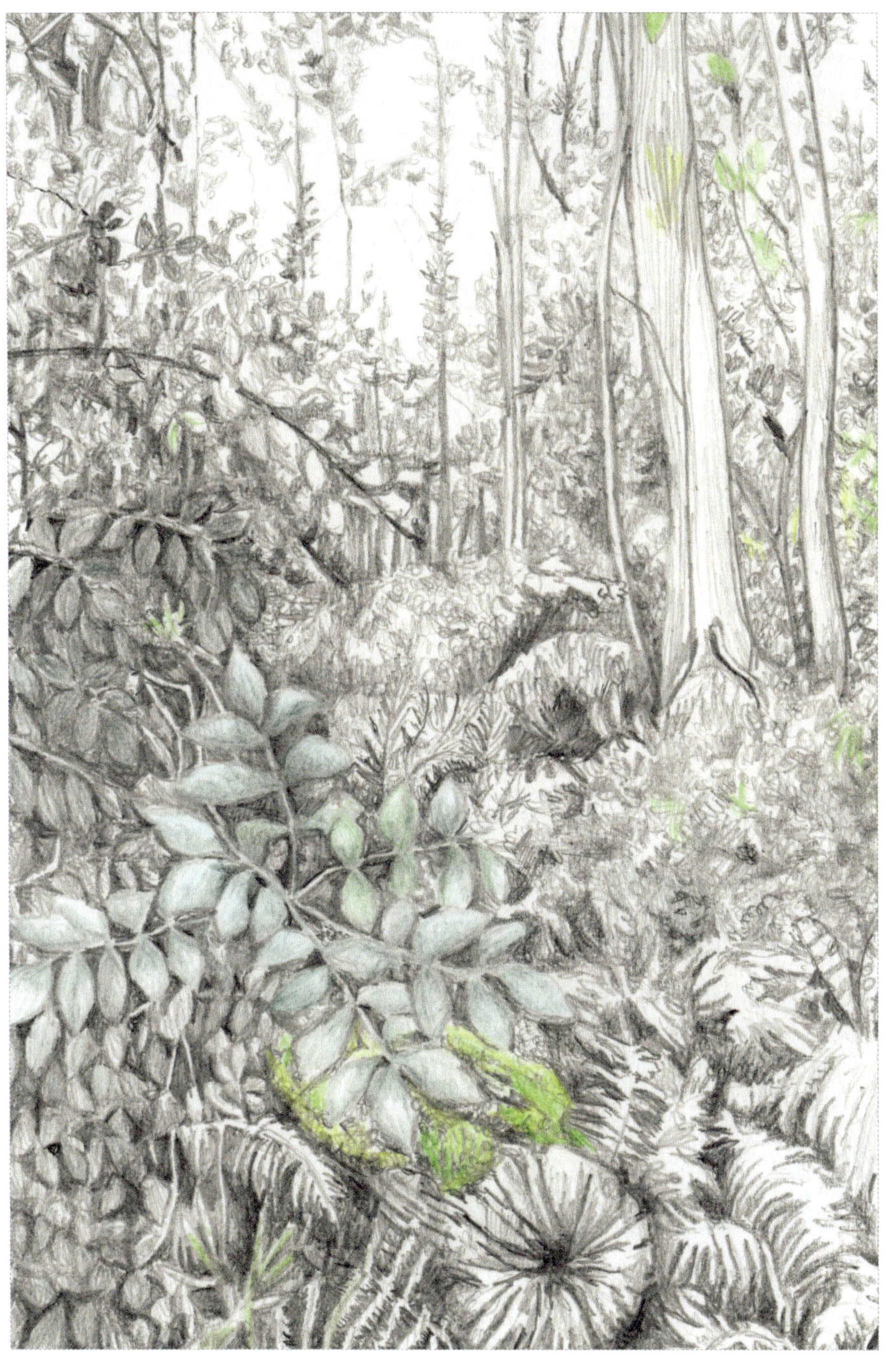

Lesson 10

Coniferous Forest

The coniferous forest is an interesting contrast to the verdant rainforest of Lesson 9. Coniferous trees typically acidify the soil, reducing the amount of ground cover compared with a broadleaf woodland or tropical rainforest, changing the character of the scene.

An artist tackling a coniferous woodland can expect to notice tall trees, few side branches, a relatively bare understorey, and high tree density – particularly in commercial plantations. This darker and less "busy" forest scene lends itself to fineliner drawings. Employing a cross-hatching technique gives a vintage, etched print feel to the finished artwork.

In this exercise, you will proceed in a similar way to the previous lesson but working into the initial sketch in fineliner rather than graphite. Take a moment to try the cross-hatching warm-up first, to get used to the technique. This drawing style can then be applied to many of the other subjects explored in the book.

Warm-up Exercise: Cross-hatching

Before you begin your sketch, try to replicate the tonal gradient below using hatching and cross-hatching. This quick exercise will help you to get used to the action of cross-hatching so that you can apply it to different tonal areas of the forest drawing.

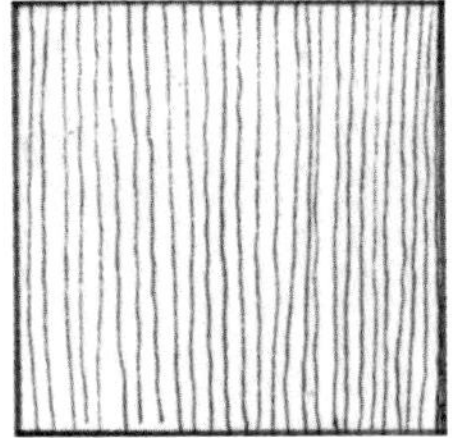

The simplest form of hatching is a series of parallel lines in a single direction. The device of spacing the lines closer together or wider apart can be used to vary the tone of your shading.

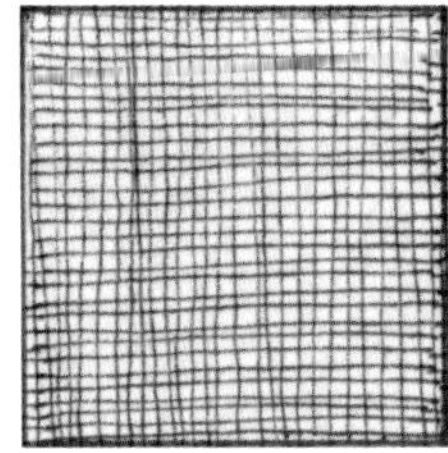

In this box, lines have been added over the top to produce a cross-hatching effect. These lines are placed 90 degrees over the initial lines and are a similar distance apart.

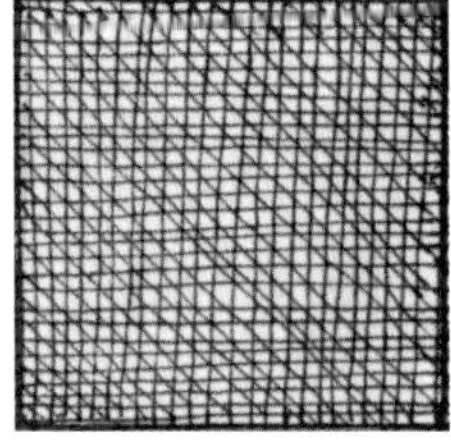

Here, a third set of lines has been added at 45 degrees to the second set, a similar distance apart. Note how the addition of these lines has further darkened the tone.

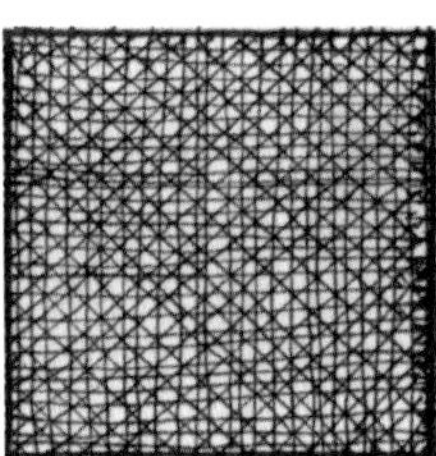

A fourth set of lines has been added at 90 degrees to the third set. All lines are spaced a similar distance apart, but together they build density of shading.

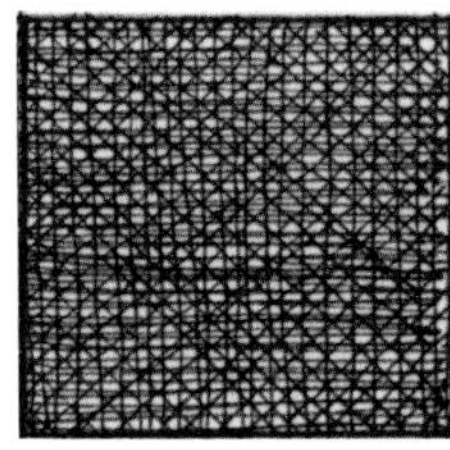

More lines have been added in all four directions to further darken the effect. Note that only four directions continue to be used: more directions would become too chaotic, but all of the lines are now closer together.

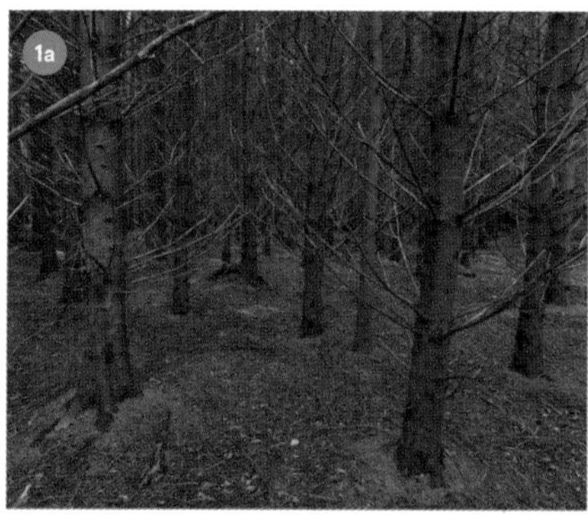

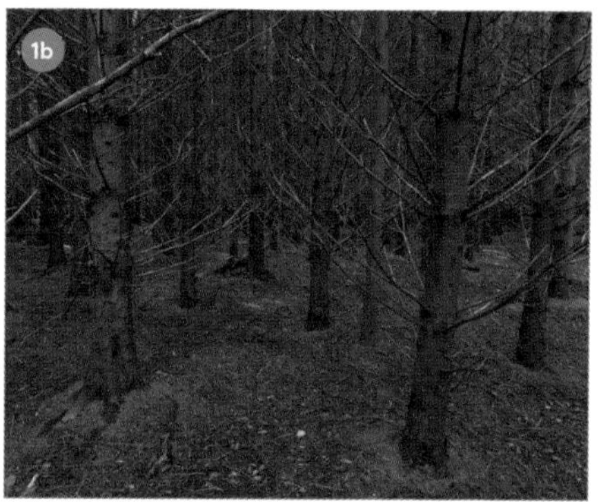

❶ Begin with a reference photo (1a) of a conifer woodland or apply these techniques to the habitat of your chosen tree. As in Lesson 9, convert your photo into greyscale (1b), either using a filter or by printing it out in black and white.

❷ Prepare a quick graphite sketch to situate the main tree trunks in the forest scene, paying attention to the location of trees in the background. Indicate the placement of any major lateral branches. Positioning the base of each background tree at the correct height relative to the trees in the foreground will help to generate perspective.

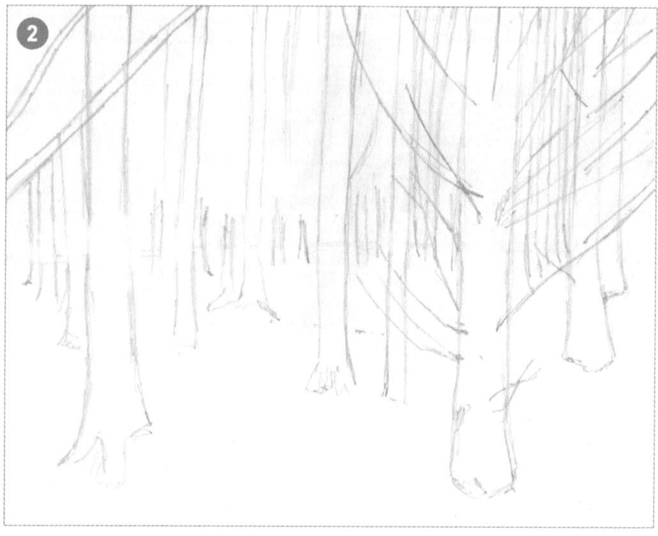

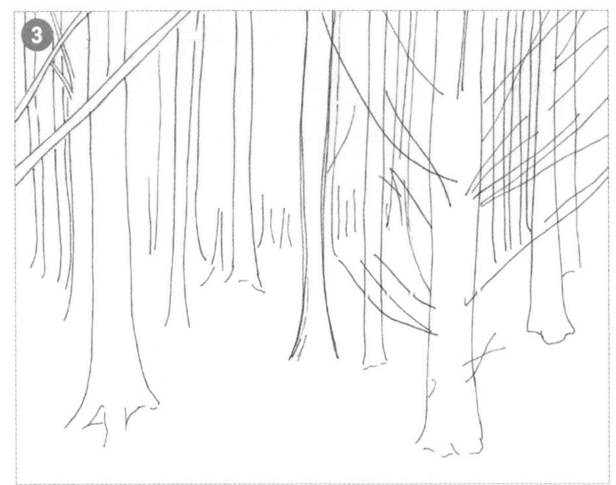

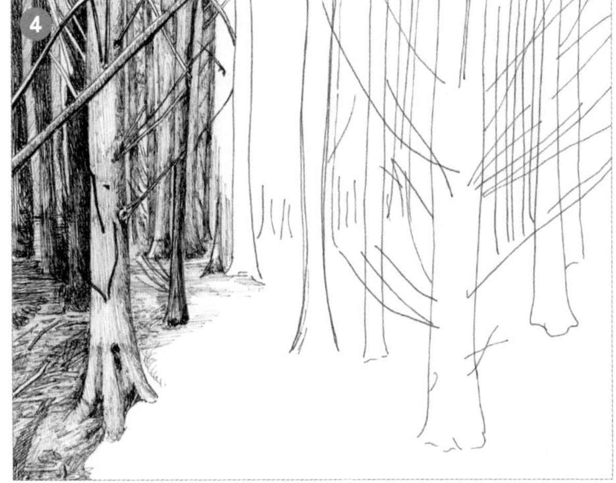

❸ Use a thick fineliner, such as 0.3, to outline the tree trunks and major branches. Once these are in place, the underlying pencil sketch can be removed with an eraser.

❹ Work from one side of your drawing to the other, starting at the left-hand side if you are right-handed, and right-hand side if you are left-handed. Use a thin fineliner, such as 0.1 and 0.05, and think about using a different line direction for each part of the scene. For example, I used a base of vertical lines for the tree trunks but horizontal lines for the forest floor.

5 On top of these initial lines, use marks in other directions to build density of shading. I have built dark shading onto the background tree trunks using strong cross-hatching. For these organic subjects, it is not necessary to use rigorous straight lines as shown in the warm-up exercise. Instead, allow some lines to follow the shape or contour of the tree trunks and branches, as shown in Lesson 2.

6 Continue to work across the drawing, filling in details one area at a time. Include more detail on individual tree trunks that are in the foreground, compared to those further away. This is also necessary for the complexity of lines on the forest floor. Adding a few sharp outlines of features, such as fallen twigs close to the front of the drawing, helps create depth.

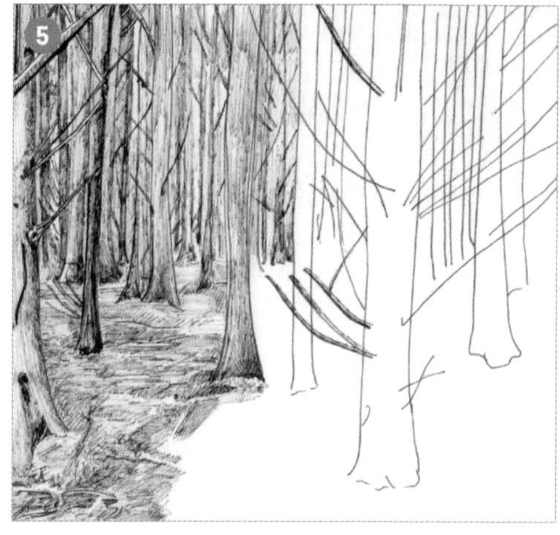

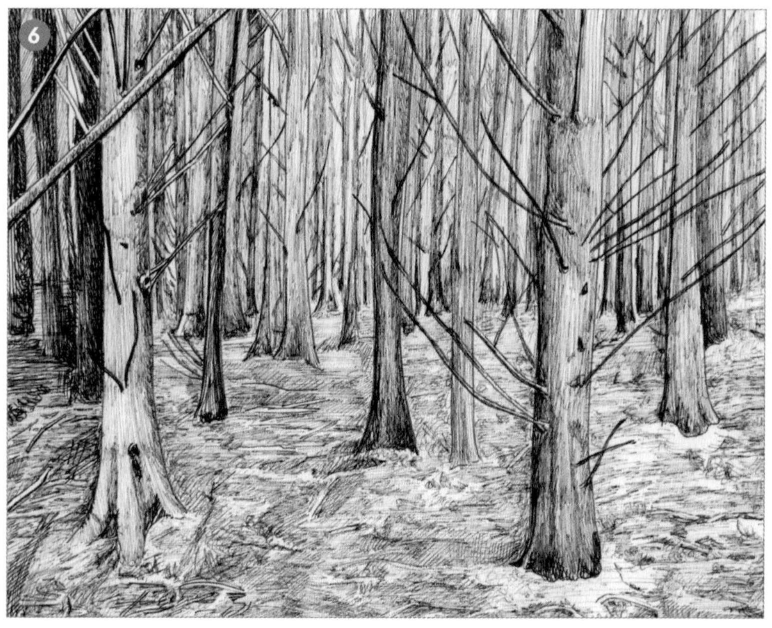

Gallery

The illustrative, etching style of this form of black fineliner illustration is especially appealing for dense forest subjects. However, it is also worth trying this technique with other fineliner colours. This conifer woodland scene was drawn with sepia fineliner in sizes 0.3 and 0.1. Note the close-up crop and focus on vertical lines for every tree trunk. All vertical lines were drawn first and then lines were added in other directions to resolve the stripy effect into a page of trees!

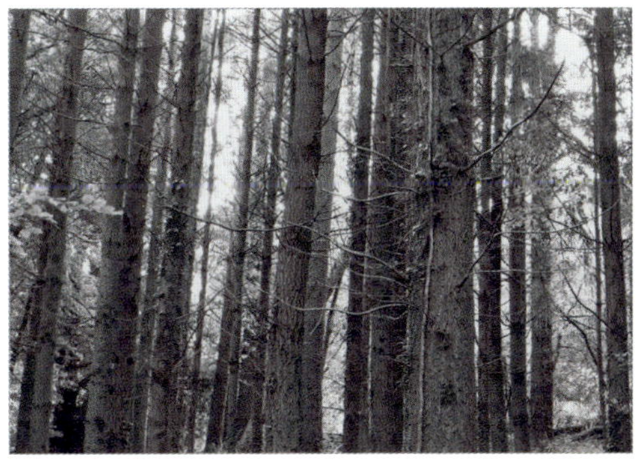

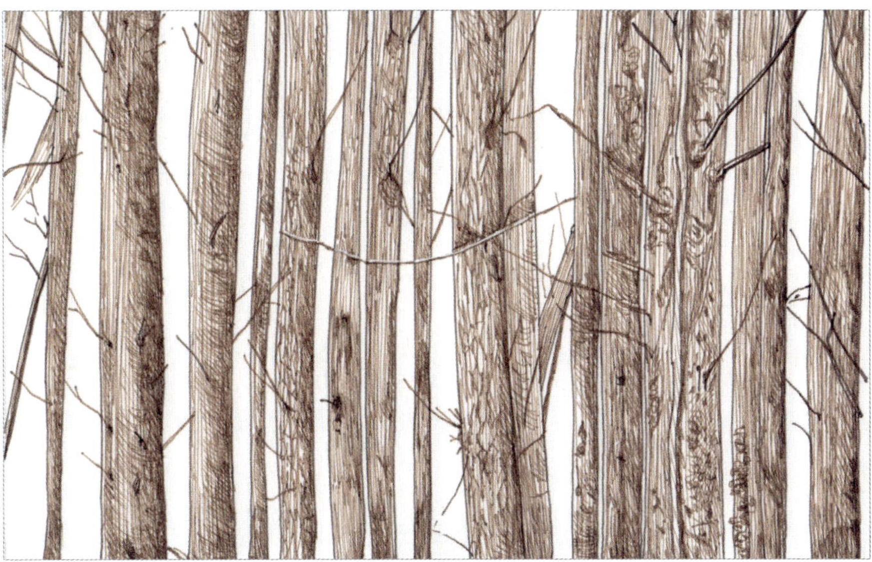

Lesson 11

Autumn Colour

The bright colours of a crisp autumn day are an immediate attraction for the artist studying trees. Most tree species that put on a good display are broadleaf deciduous types, although some coniferous trees, such as larches, also change colour and drop their needles as the season changes.

If your tree is deciduous, autumn is an excellent time to really notice the leaves change. Start to observe the shifts in colour and condition of the leaves from the end of the summer, and watch to see how the leaves gradually turn within the tree as a whole.

Capturing the broad range of autumnal red-yellow hues in a woodland scene is a great way to practise layering and blending techniques with coloured pencil. In this exercise, we will look at drawing effective autumn colour displays, building from the graphite techniques at the start of the chapter.

Additional material:

Burnisher pencil (optional)

1 Take a photo of your tree in autumn colour or use a reference photo that has a good range of different colours, preferably a woodland or forest scene. Another option is to focus in on the colourful leaves, with a detailed close-up, as shown in the Gallery example. I have chosen a Japanese maple woodland and have angled the camera to look through the canopies of several trees.

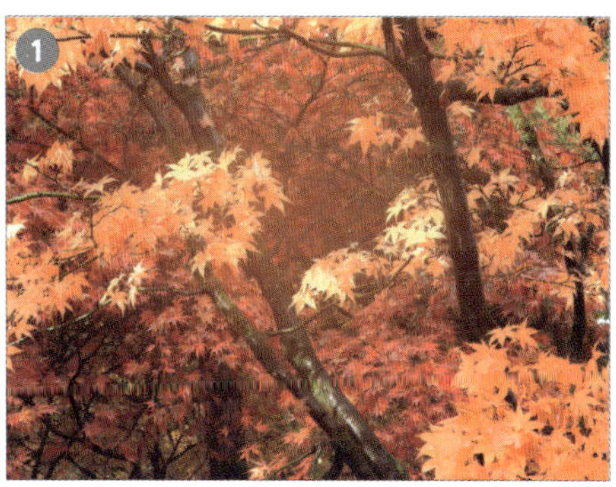

2 Begin with a graphite sketch to position the main clusters of leaves and the most important branches. As described in Lesson 1, look for "clouds" of leaves and draw an outline of each of these areas at this stage.

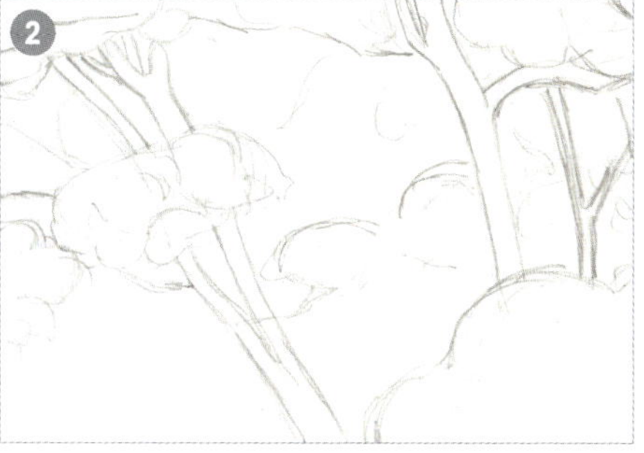

3 Add some suggestions of leaf shape to your "leaf cloud" clusters. The studies made of your tree in your nature journal will help you, so you should be more familiar with your tree's leaves now. I chose to do this stage in sepia fineliner (0.1) and then removed the pencil lines below, although this is optional. If you retain the graphite, ensure that any extra lines used to map out your leaf clusters are now removed.

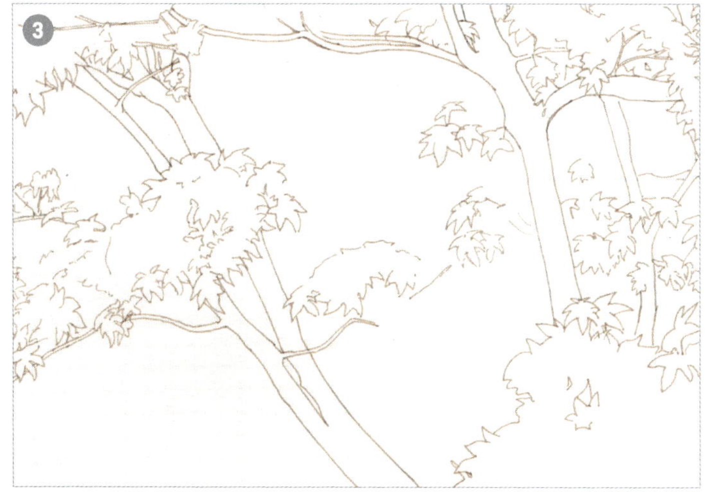

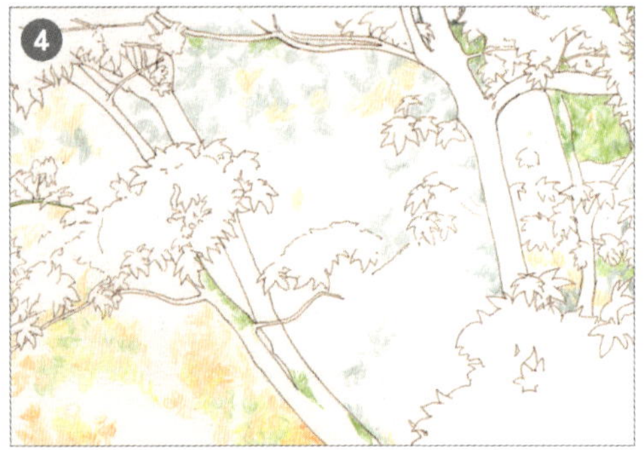

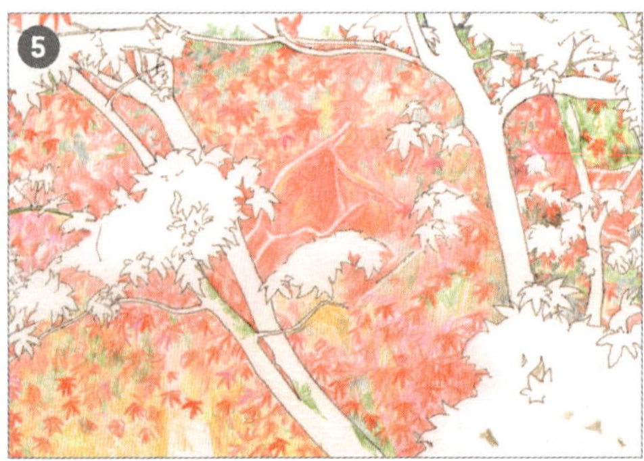

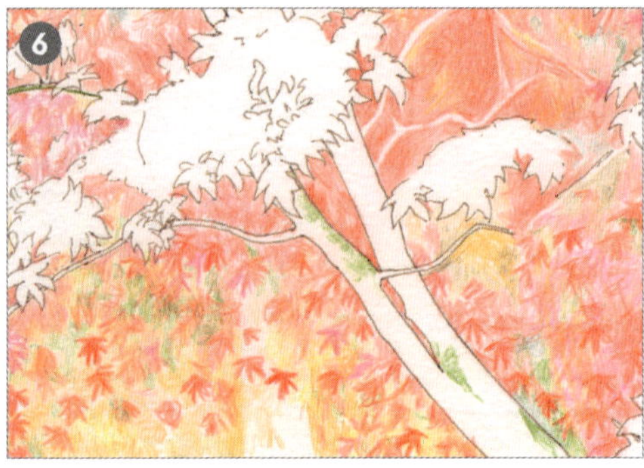

❹ Look deep into the background of your photograph and select the colours of the most distant features. I noticed areas of green and yellow leaves in my reference, so filled these in with a soft, circular motion of my pencil. Even at this stage, try to suggest the distant leaf shapes.

❺ Add areas of colour, working from the furthest leaves to the closest. Use a spare sheet of paper under your hand to avoid smudging. Layering the coloured pencil, rather than working from one side to the other as we did in Lesson 9, allows colours to build naturally, becoming stronger in the foreground.

❻ As you work on closer subjects, start to add details of individual leaves here and there in prominent positions. Use your reference photo as a guide – where can you see the shapes of leaves most clearly? These work best in areas of high contrast with the background colour. Ensure you use a sharp pencil for these little details.

7 Continue to build up the layers, leaving the closest leaves for the final stage. Add colours to the tree trunks, building in layers (lightest colours first) and noticing on which side of the trunks and branches the shadows are located. Look at your reference photo for areas of strongest colour and apply denser shading here.

8 Add in the closest leaves, using a sharp pencil to give these the greatest variation in contrast, detail, and depth. Optionally, give your drawing a final layer of "burnisher" pencil or a light colour from your set (pale yellows, skin tones, and rose pinks) to blend the colours together and give that final shine (see Lesson 3, Burnishing).

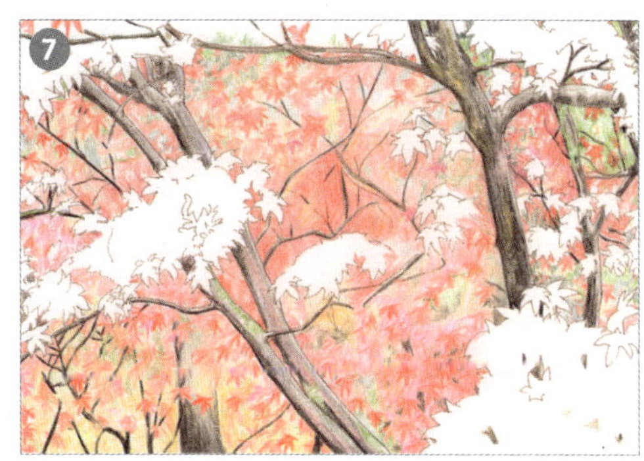

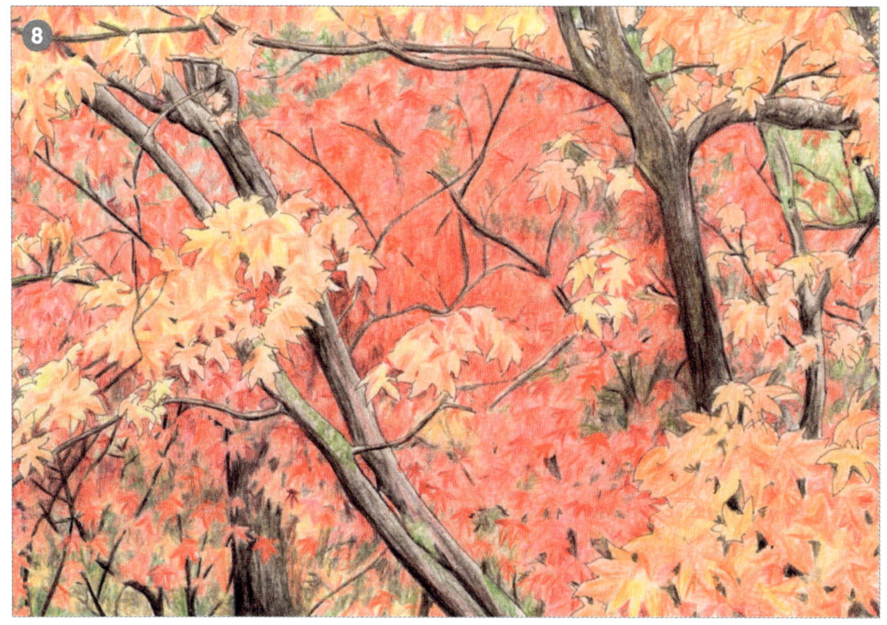

Gallery

Autumn leaves are also beautiful viewed a little closer up. This reference photo was taken from the same group of Japanese maple trees but at a tighter angle. Here, I used a similar approach to the broader scene, adding the most distant colours first and increasing the density of light, shadow, and details such as veins on the closest leaves. Some areas were left close to the colour of the paper to replicate highlights and indicate the glossy shine of the wet leaves.

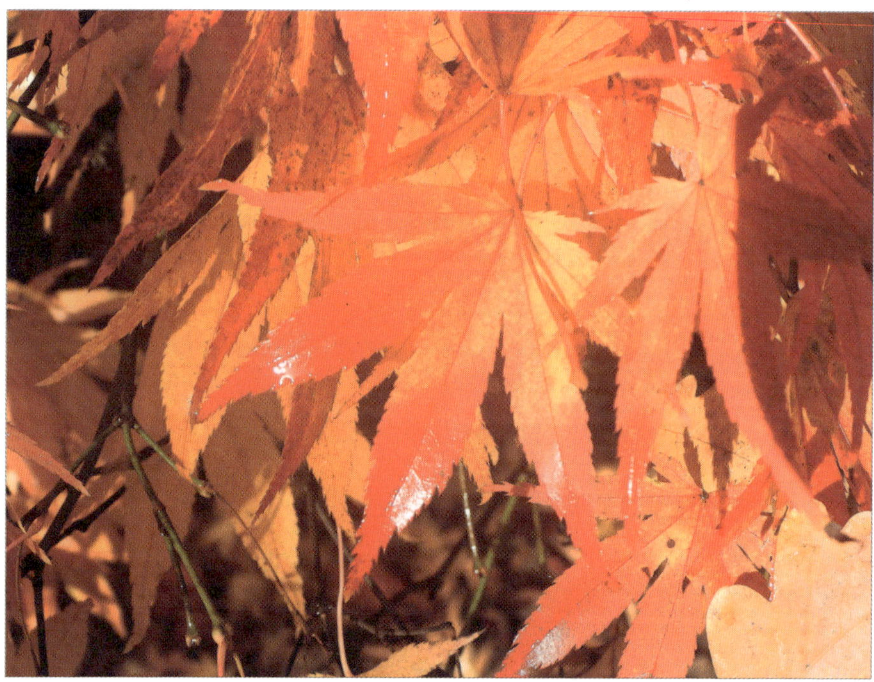

TIP:

Remember that your artwork is always that – an artistic representation of reality, filtered through you and your experience. We do not need to aim for a drawing resembling a photographic representation, otherwise we may as well just frame the reference photograph! Instead, look for the aspects of the subject or your reference photograph that made you choose it to work from in the first place. In this case, I was taken by the rich colours of the shadows on the leaves and so I deliberately emphasised these in the final work, leaving other areas with lower contrast than present in the reference image.

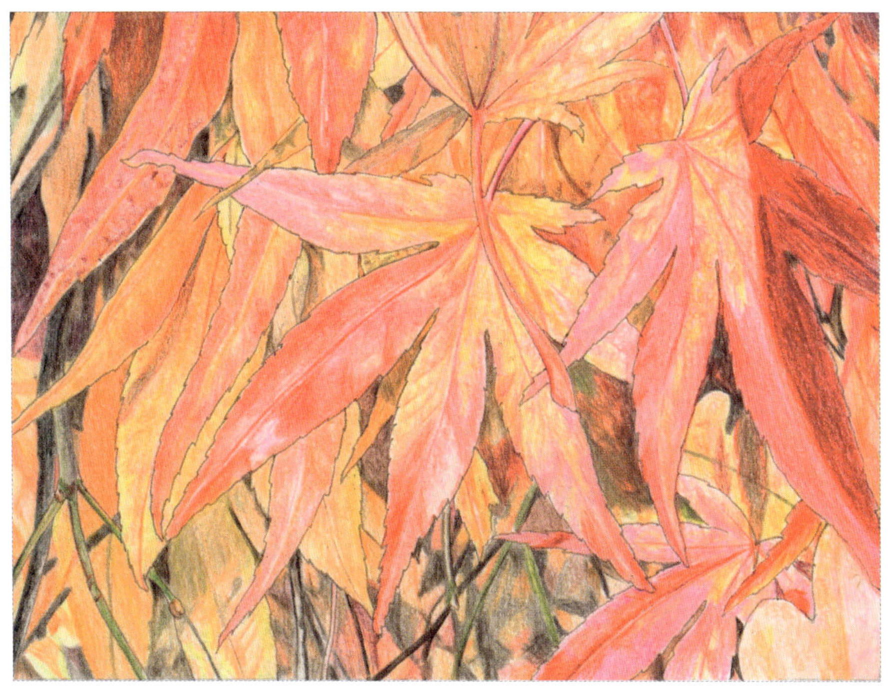

Lesson 12

Layered Landscape

Trees are an important feature of many of the landscapes we know and love, from the sweep of mountain forests to the urban promenade. When nature journaling or sketchbooking, consider how your chosen tree fits into its landscape. Think of whether its position is natural or decided by humans, and how the wider environs have shaped, and been shaped by, the presence of the tree.

Creating an artwork to position your tree in its surroundings can be challenging. When composing a photograph or drawing, consider how far away you can reach to set your tree in context but still keep it visible and recognisable. Think of this as an interesting photography or compositional challenge and try a few different ideas before settling on a location.

The differences in tone and colour provided by a whole landscape often favour the dramatic. The most impactful way I have found to convey theses variations is to use different paper tones. In this exercise, I show you how to use toned papers with coloured pencils to emphasise the variety in the landscape.

Additional materials:

Coloured papers, scissors, craft knife, cutting mat, EVA glue, paintbrush

❶ Take your reference photo and look for distinct areas in the scene that could be easily defined by different papers. In this hillside forest, I noticed three areas: the most distant trees on the hill, the central ridge sloping from left to right, and the brightly lit trees and hillside in the foreground.

❷ Select your papers. Using a pair of scissors, roughly cut the papers into the shape of your landscape areas, leaving plenty of space to later cut away around details. You might prefer to draw a quick pencil guide first to outline each section.

❸ Allowing plenty of space below the upper edge of each piece, add a graphite drawing of the main elements of the scene. If you are working on a dark paper, use a white colouring pencil for this stage. Do a quick sketch on the underlying layers to map where each paper will overlap so that you know where to fill in with your more detailed colouring.

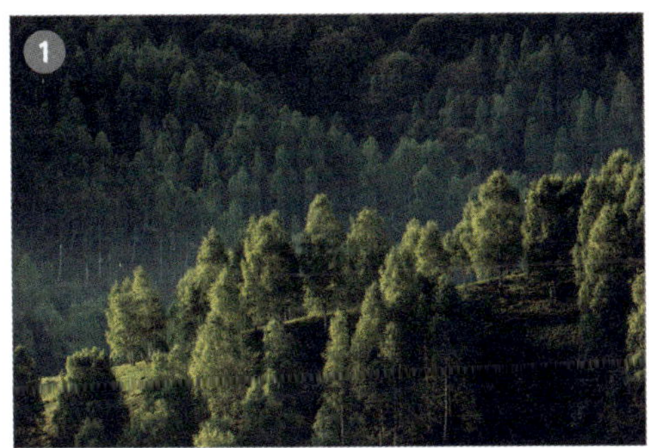

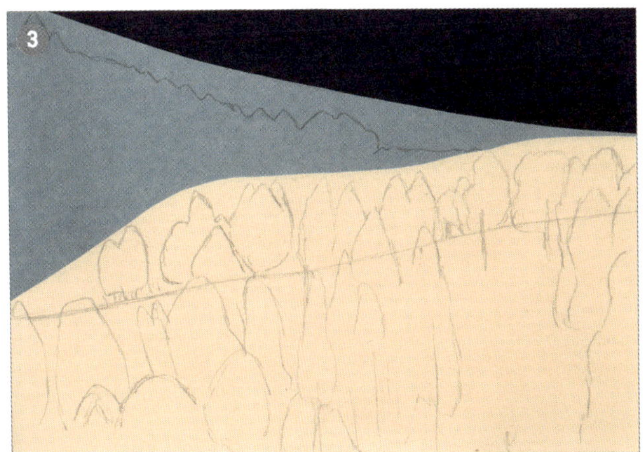

TIP:

A range of coloured papers can be purchased from art suppliers, including black, dark blue, kraft (brown), natural (tan), grey, and verdigris green. Ensure your chosen paper is suitable for use with coloured pencil.

❹ Begin the coloured pencil work on your bottom-most layer. Use suggestions of shapes and loose outlines to represent details in the furthest distance. I drew a guide line to help me decide where the next layer would overlap. Be generous with your colouring work and extend the drawing a little lower than necessary, to avoid any blank space if you accidentally trim one of the upper layers too low.

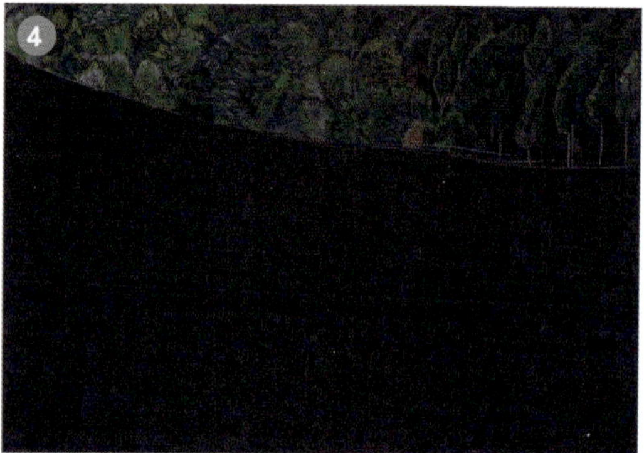

❺ Work on the next layer of paper, emphasising areas of light and shade, as this layer is a little closer to the viewer. Note how the lighter tonal ground shifts the visual effect of the coloured pencil work, even though the colours used are very similar to the first layer.

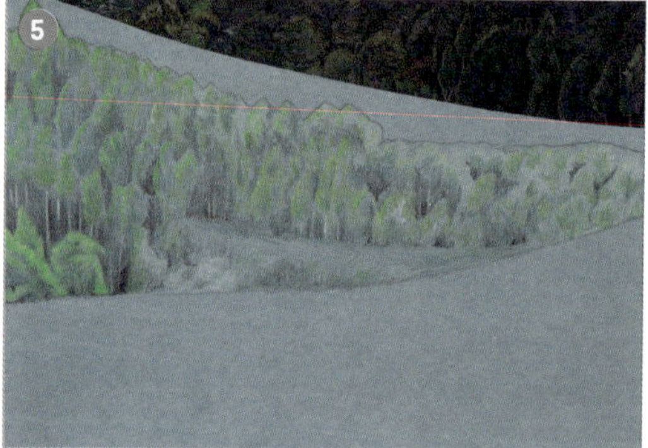

❻ For your closest, top, layer, add more details to the scene, such as the tree trunks and textures on the hillside in my drawing. Your foreground layer may also have the most complex level of cutting out required, increasing the degrees of intricacy and interest at the front of the picture, helping to push this forward and add to the sense of depth in the landscape.

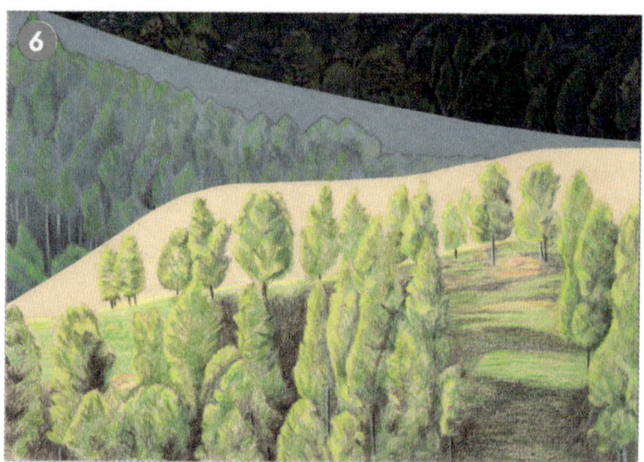

7 Once the coloured pencil work is finished, it is time to cut out your finished layers more accurately. If you have one, a sharp craft knife and self-healing cutting mat are ideal for this, although good effects can be achieved by careful cutting with a pair of scissors. Cut each layer separately and lay them together regularly to check your progress.

8 Finally, when all the cutting is finished, add a layer of EVA glue to the back of each layer and carefully position the layers together to assemble the final drawing. I recommend EVA glue for collage work as it is flexible and pH neutral.

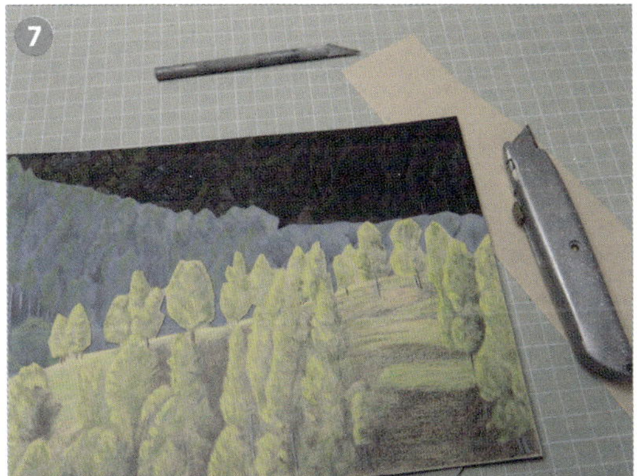

TIP:

Use a paintbrush to apply glue and place the layer on newspaper or scrap paper to ensure you can add glue all the way to the edges.

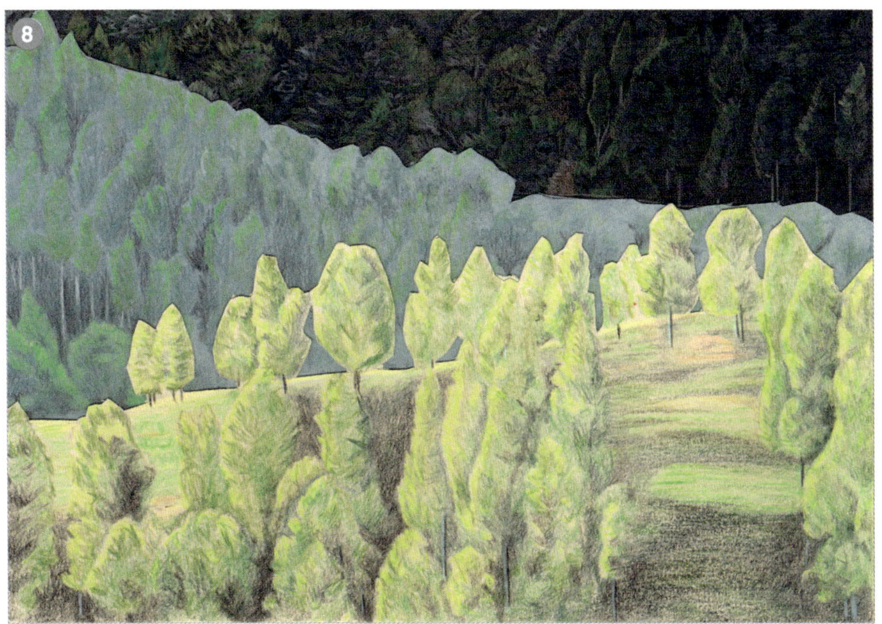

Gallery

Don't feel limited by the number of layers or paper colours you can use in this method – have fun and experiment! Five layers of paper (in three colours) were used to build my version of this hillside. Notice how I carefully cut the paper to match the features of the landscape and added strong coloured pencil details as I layered the papers together. A textured, white watercolour paper produced a wintery sky.

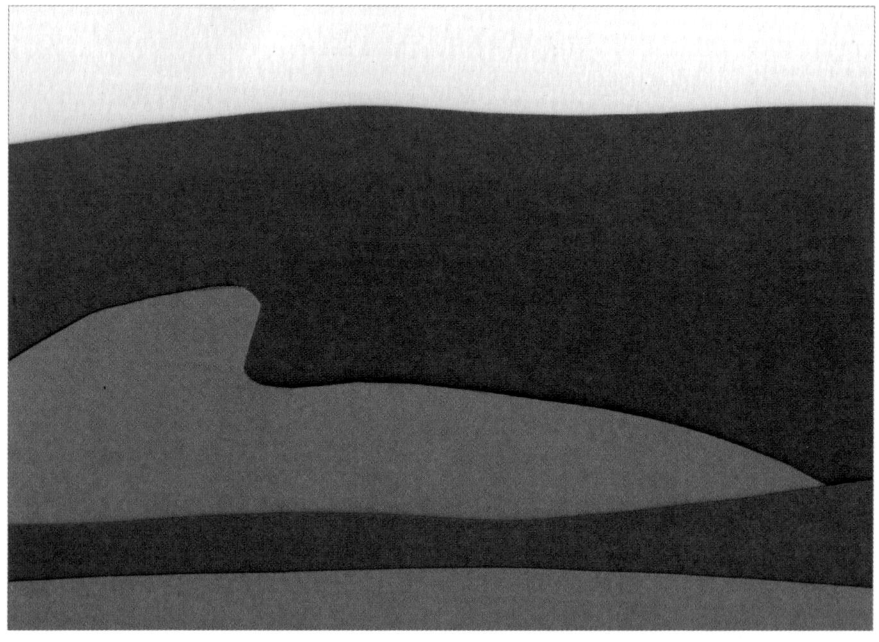

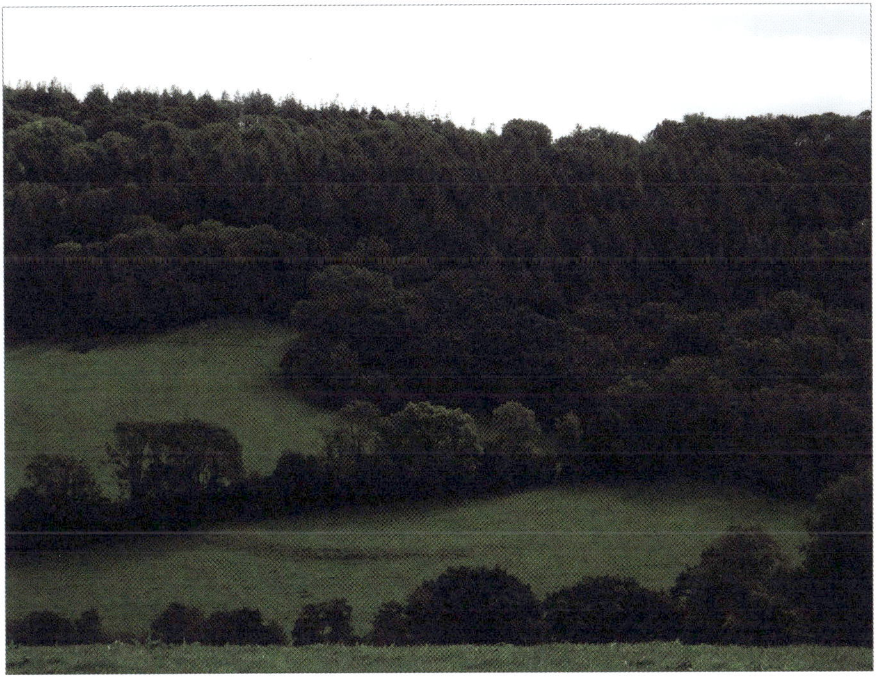

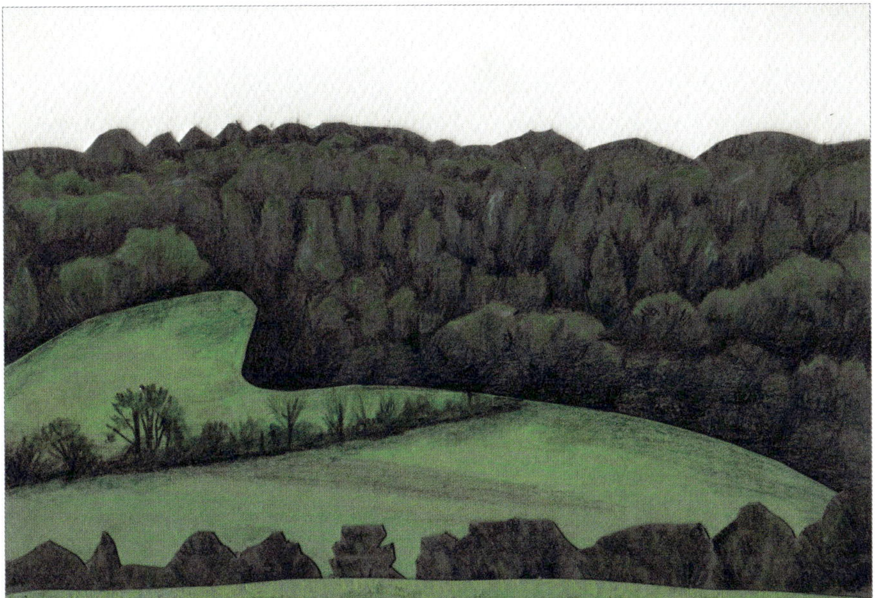

Chapter 4

Reimagining Trees

It's time to approach your creative process from different perspectives. This chapter will encourage you to break away from traditional practices, using abstraction to discover the beauty of natural patterns found on your tree and exploring nature in urban environments. Gathering found materials outdoors to use in a collage is a great way to connect your tree directly into your artwork.

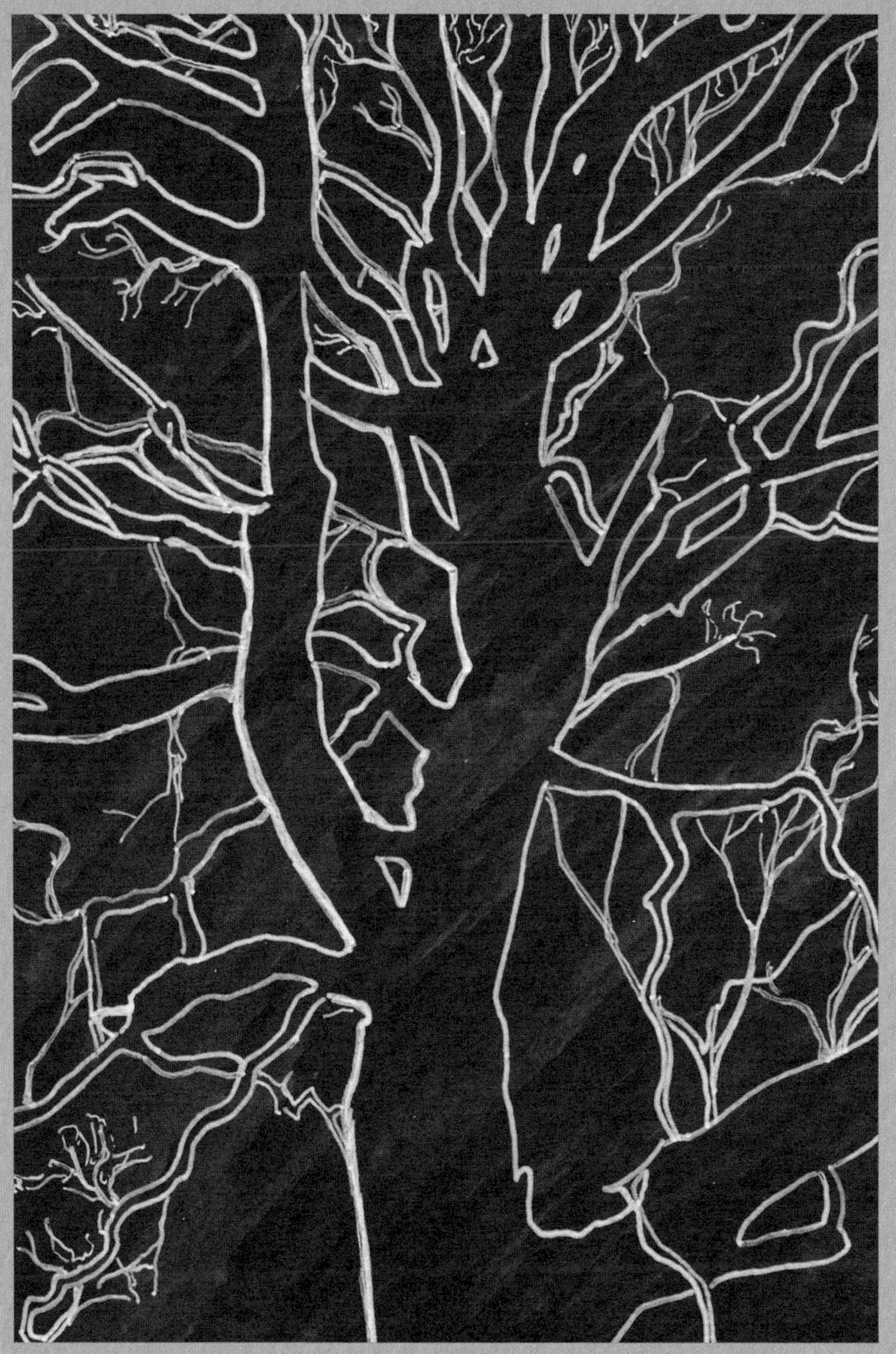

Lesson 13

Bark Abstraction

Bark is one of the most distinctive features by which to tell trees apart and is well worth a close inspection. The variety of colours and textures, plus the common presence of other organisms such as mosses, lichens, and fungi, give great potential for having some artistic fun with tones and shapes.

Take a close look at the bark of your chosen tree, or a selection of trees in your woodland. Features of the bark can tell us a lot about the tree – its "skin" bears scars of past events and, for some trees, the thickness of ridges can give a hint as to the tree's age. It is interesting to see how the bark varies around the trunk and with height.

For the first time, we will look past the immediate and try extending our artistic creativity into the abstract, taking the bark patterns of your tree as a starting point. Looking at the details that make your tree's bark special, you will then simplify these into forms of shape and colour that stand artistically on their own.

Warm-up Exercise: A Continuous Line

Begin with a photo of your tree bark taken from close up (to fill the entire picture) or try using the plane tree reference photo here for this quick exercise. You will need a blank sheet of paper and a thick fineliner (I used 1.2, and added 0.8 for the cracks).

Keeping your pen down on the paper as much as possible, draw any interesting shapes you notice in the bark as a continuous, fluid line. Spend more time looking at the reference image than at your drawing and try to let the shapes you see guide the movement of your arm. This is an excellent way to focus on just the lines and shapes present. I added the broken, linear cracks with a fine line to contrast with the solid flowing shapes.

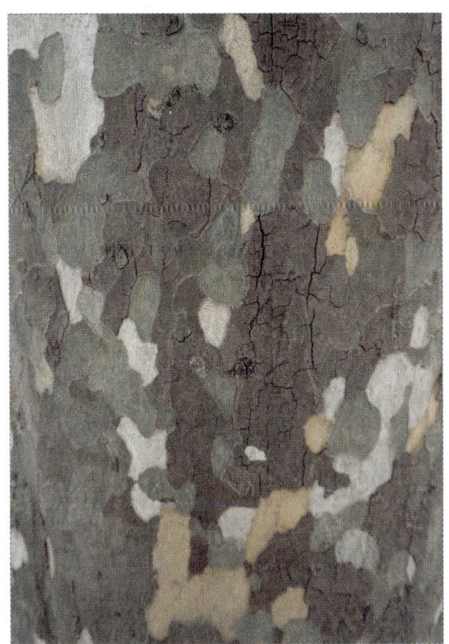

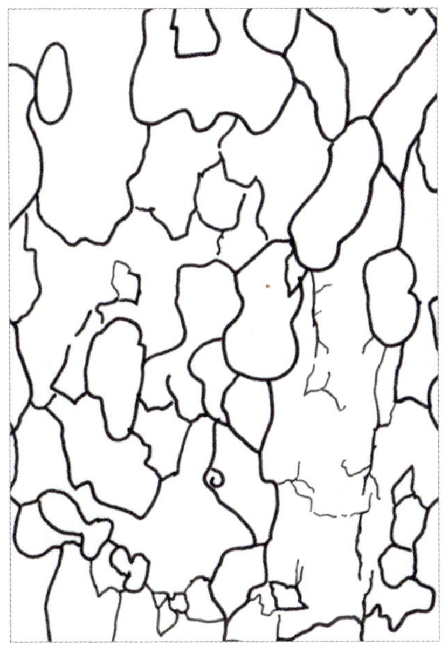

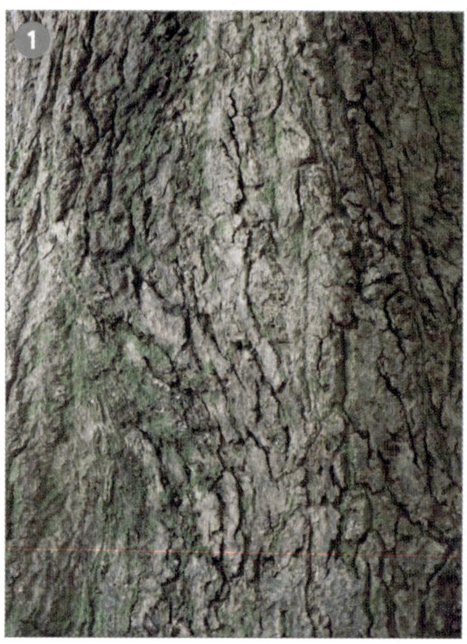

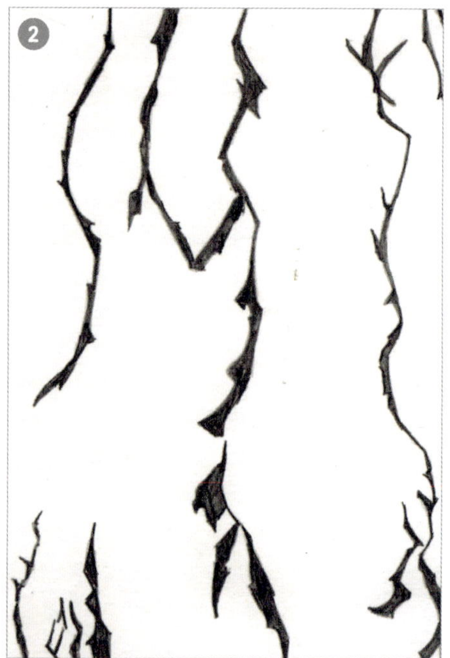

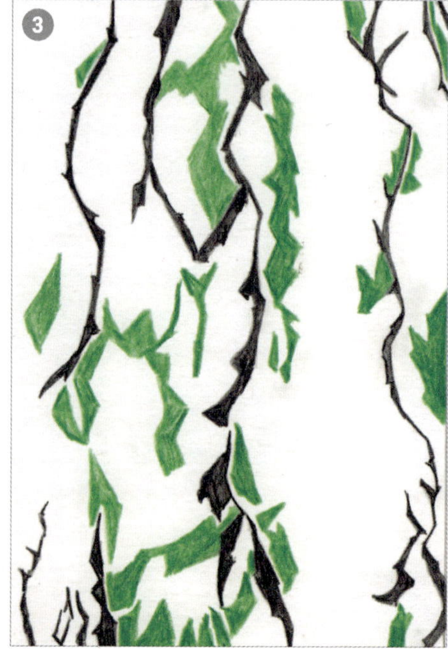

❶ For this abstraction exercise we will use coloured pencils alone to build up the shapes that we have observed in the bark photograph. My example here is an old oak tree with deep ridges in the bark and lots of green algae or moss.

❷ Pick out one interesting colour first. I chose to begin with the bold, dark cracks between the ridges of the bark, so selected a strong black. Whichever colour is present, try to exaggerate it. Simplify the many shades visible in the bark into one dynamic representation.

❸ Select a second colour and add another set of shapes. I chose to focus on the areas of green next. By simplifying the bark into these sets of shapes and colours, I found I noticed more about the position and texture of the green organism growing on the bark surface.

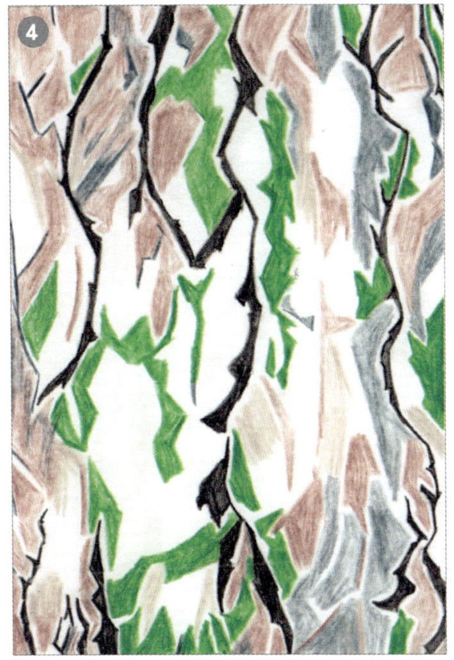

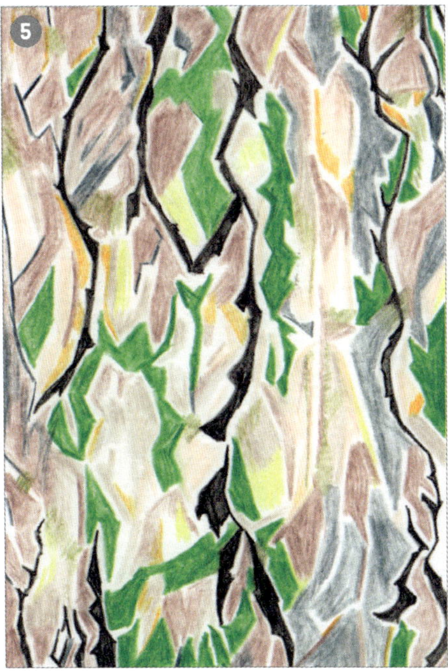

4 Continue to work with different colours. I looked closely at the reference photograph and noticed areas of red and blue, particularly where the glossy outer layer of the bark had cracked. As a contrast to the strong green and black, I chose softer, earthier reds and blues.

5 Fill out the rest of the drawing until all colours of interest to you have been represented. I chose to describe the ridges below the cracked outer bark layers in a yellow ochre. Don't be afraid to leave areas the colour of the paper. These white edges around some of the colour patches help create a three-dimensional effect of the tree bark ridges. Excessive uniformity is sometimes the enemy of an abstracted study. I blended patches of olive green across some sections to add a little variation. You might be braver and try doing this with a bright, contrasting colour!

Gallery

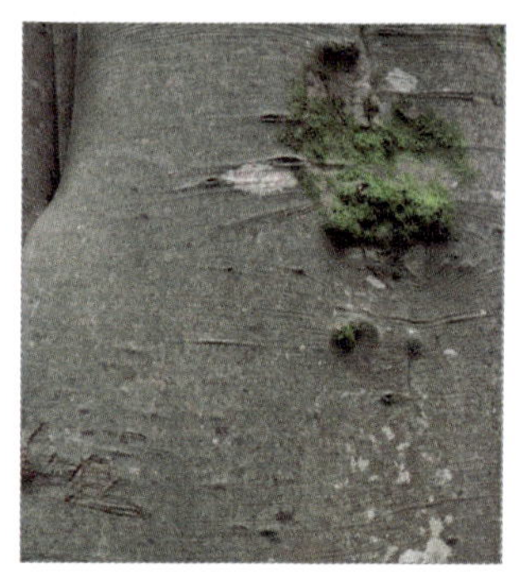

I made a feature of the eyelike markings on this birch tree trunk. I also noticed that the tree's bark was wrinkled, as though it were too tight. In the coloured pencil drawing, I emphasised these features with strong black lines then played with patches of colour to represent the lichens and mosses.

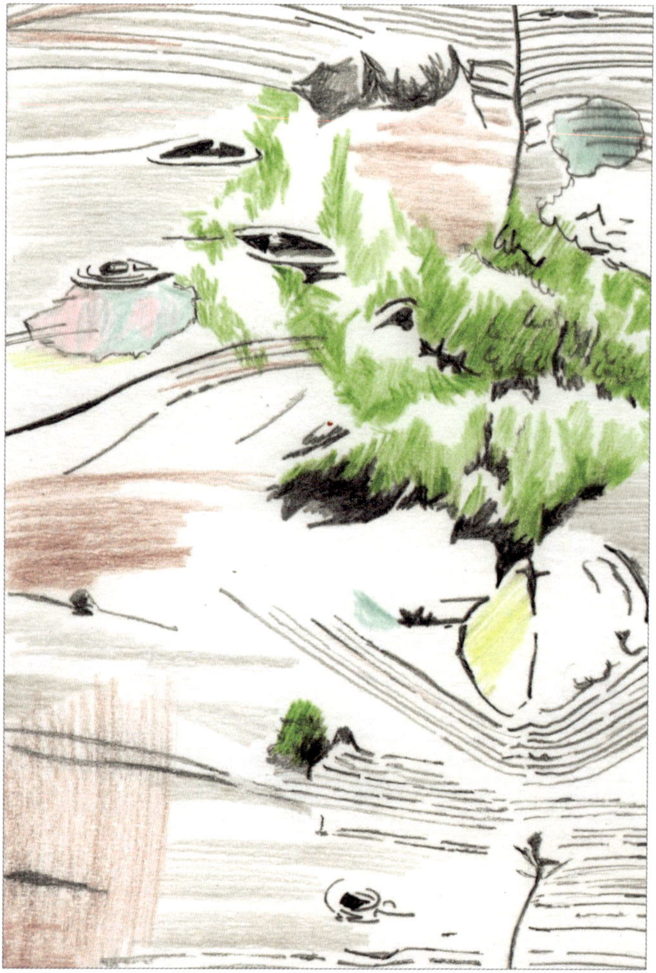

It is not always necessary to abstract fully. Filling a page, or a box drawn onto the page, with a representation of the texture of the tree trunk is an interesting simplification of the full tree. The rendering of this plane tree bark is more realistic but lacks the cylindrical effect of the tree trunk, instead being drawn as though it were perfectly flat

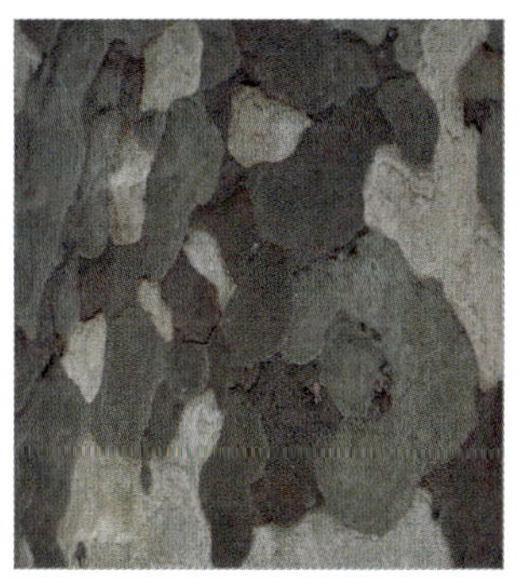

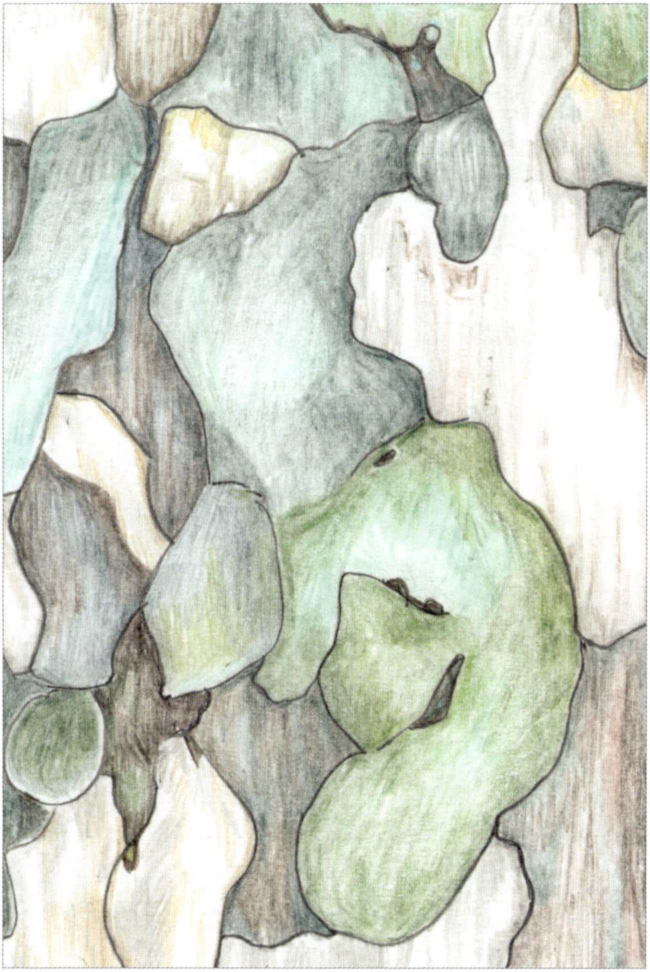

Lesson 14

Urban Trees

When drawing trees in a city setting, the biggest decision is how much of the urban environment to include in the drawing. Experiment with compositions, setting the tree in the context of its built surroundings – if you do not include some suggestion of the buildings around the tree, much of that urban context will be lost.

Even without buildings, some tree features might hint at a city setting: they may have an unusual canopy shape due to pruning or growing in the shade of buildings. They may also emerge from the ground in unusual ways, with stones or tarmac surrounding their trunk, or they may be enclosed by a fence or bench.

In this exercise, we will build on the fineliner techniques developed in earlier chapters. A range of different marks will be used to distinguish the trees from their background setting, editing the buildings and their positions to bring context to the scene.

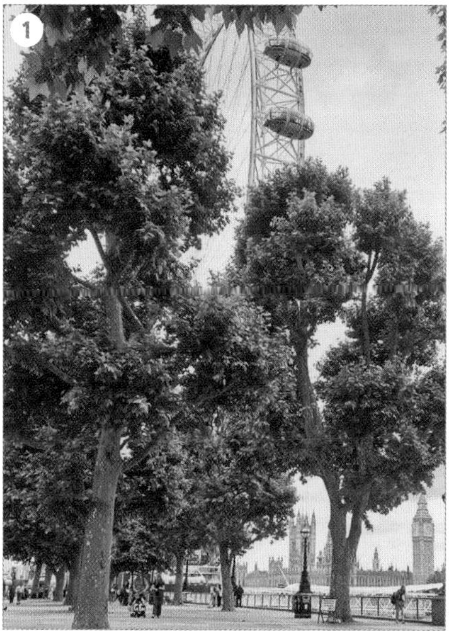

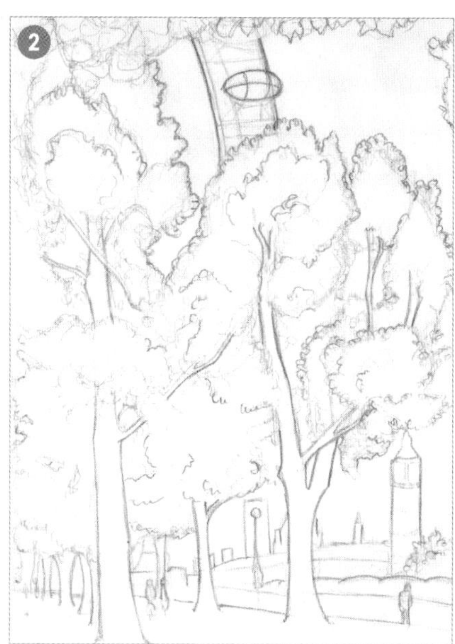

❶ Choose your reference photograph. As in earlier exercises, to help you find the tonal values of the drawing, convert your reference photo to greyscale or mono on screen, or print it out in black and white.

❷ First, sketch out your overall scene in pencil. At this stage, work out how much of the buildings surrounding the urban tree you would like to include. In this example, the trees were positioned by the river with iconic landmark buildings in the distance. I chose to include all the buildings, but kept the emphasis on the trees as the main subject.

❸ Now use black fineliner pens to give everything a basic outline, starting with the trunks and closer leaves. Use the finest pens for the most distant or smallest elements, and change to thicker pens for dominant or closer subjects.

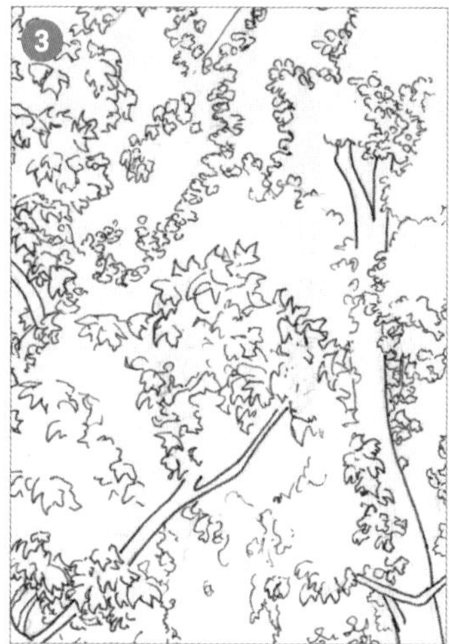

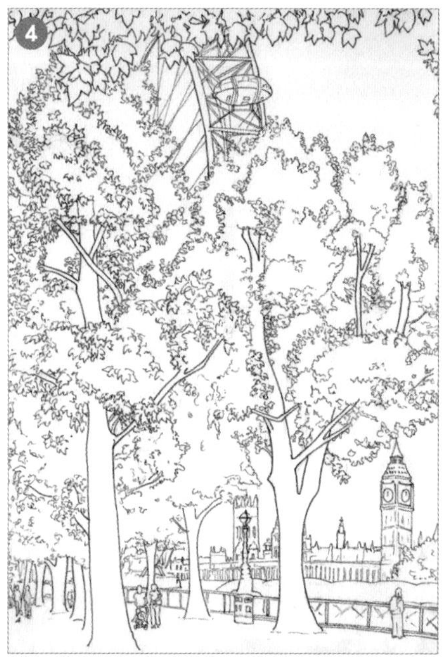

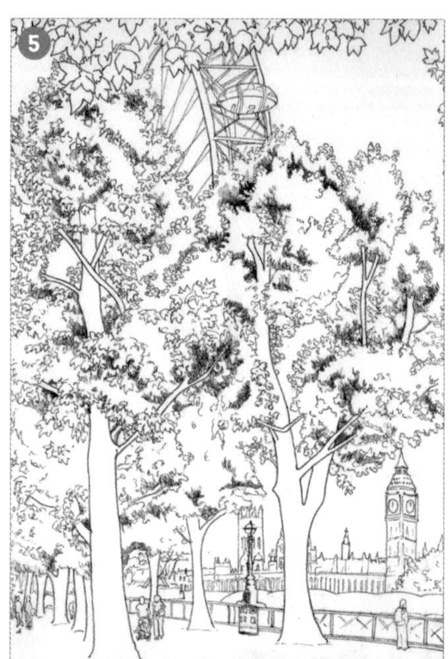

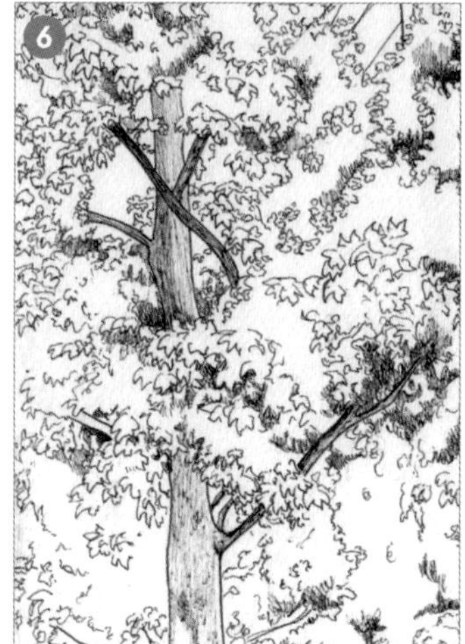

4 When working on the leaves, use information gathered about your tree to help guide your marks. What shape are the leaves? On the closer branches, use your knowledge of the leaf shape to delineate some leaves. This will give your tree its particular "likeness". Notice how the leaves all sit at different angles and incorporate this into your sketch. Make the leaves less distinct on branches further from the viewer and on distant trees.

5 Remove the pencil lines with a pointed or battery-operated eraser to give a clean ink-only drawing. At this stage, the image is reduced to its main components, using stronger lines to give weight to the trees as the primary subject.

6 To build depth and detail, fill in the very darkest areas of the foliage with a series of denser marks. You could start with the lines all facing a single direction, and then cross over with lines in an opposing direction to build tone. Or, you might prefer a less rigid approach using looser hatching. Refer to your greyscale photo to help you find these dark patches.

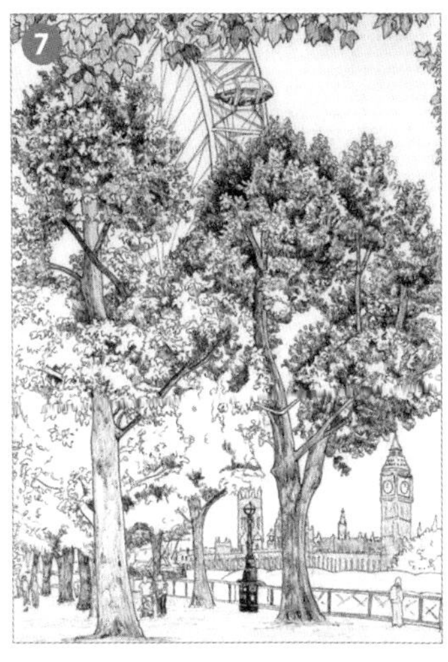

7 Use different line types and directions for different parts of the picture. A long up-and-down, regular stroke was used for the tree trunks, which contrasts with the shorter and rougher marks used in the foliage.

8 Continue to use line shading to help differentiate between closer and more distant objects, as well as darker and lighter objects. Narrow, widely spaced lines are used to add a touch of tonal contrast to the buildings in the background. Dense shading with a thicker fineliner is used for solid foreground features, such as the lamp post. Keep building out the foliage, making sure that some lighter areas remain white for contrast.

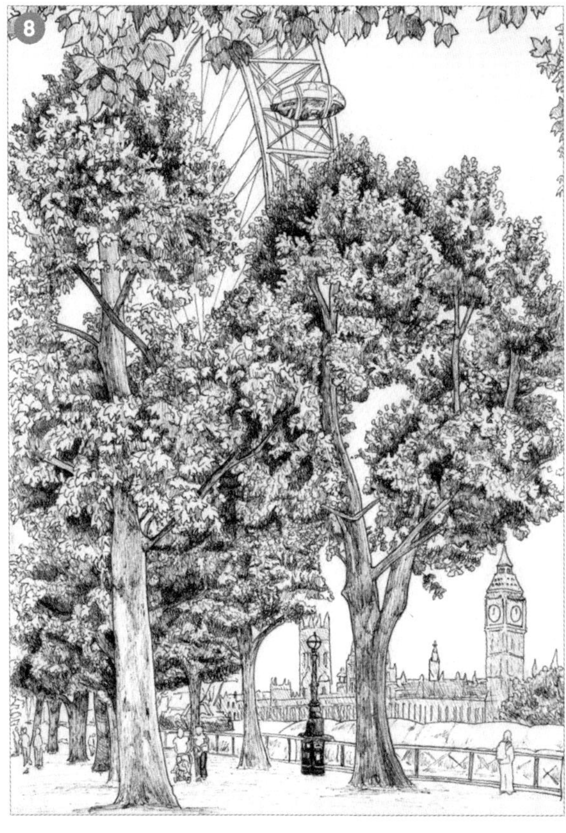

Gallery

This tree has been drastically pruned, resulting in a very interesting canopy structure. Notice that the buildings in the background have been heavily edited in the drawing and not all details are included. The lamp post on the right and partial tree trunk on the left, have also been removed to ensure that the tree is promoted as the main subject of the artwork.

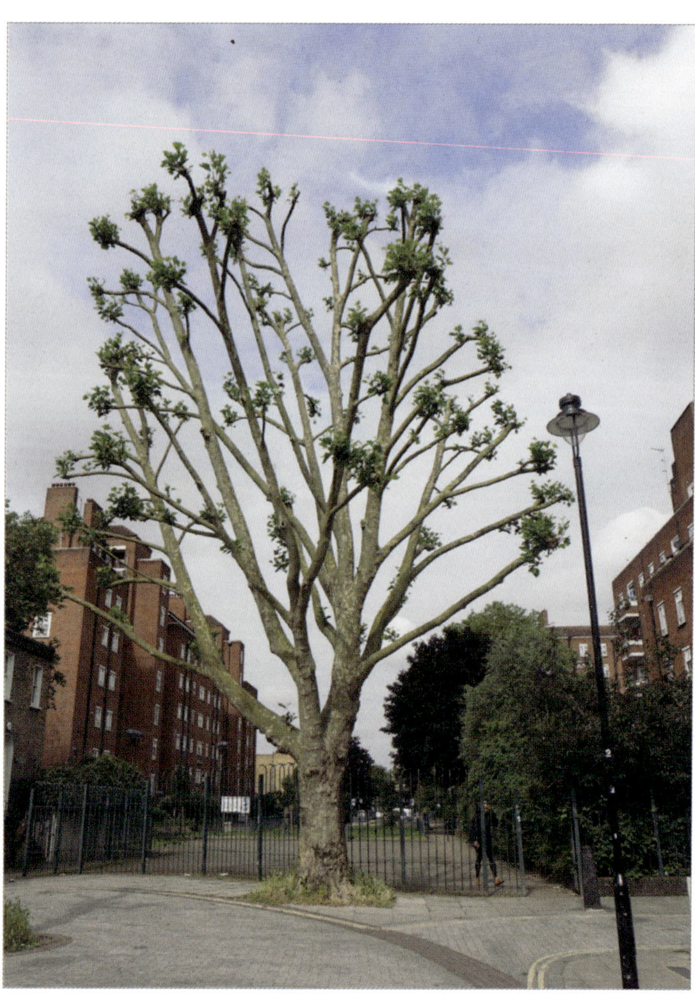

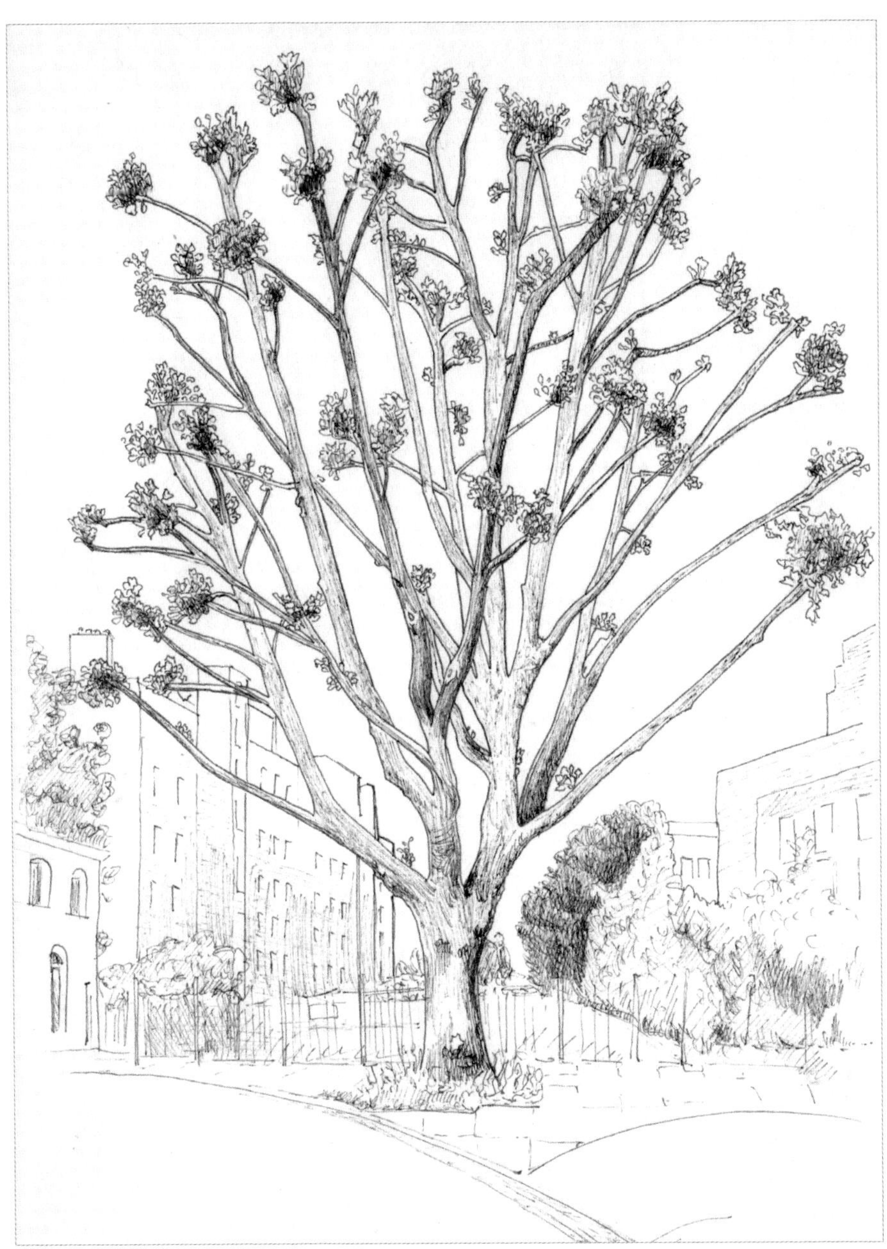

Lesson 15

Tree Frames

One very effective way to make drawings in a sketchbook is to hand-draw and fill several "frames". This isolates a subject on the page and gives each tree sketch a neat boundary, which can be crossed by leaves and branches to good effect. These frame drawings can also work well displayed on the wall or as greetings cards or other gifts.

You can explore the branching structure of the tree to fill the frame, or take individual elements such as leaves or branches, and then allow them to break free over the edge. This approach offers you the opportunity to take smaller and smaller sections of a tree to focus on in more detail, perhaps creating a series for your tree at different times of year.

The format of these exercises is just a guide. You could try making frames with shapes other than boxes, perhaps circles or triangles, and drawing your tree emerging from these frames. Collaged elements could also be incorporated, such as a return to the tonal papers of Lesson 12. Enjoy experimenting with this idea in your tree sketchbook.

Additional materials:

Black ink brush pen or black ink and paintbrush, white gel pen, ruler

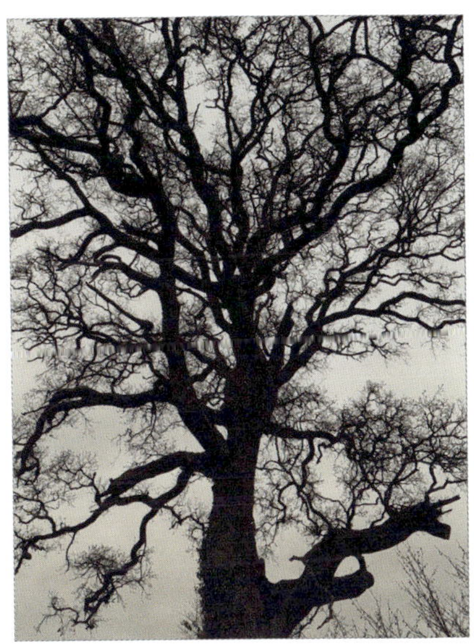

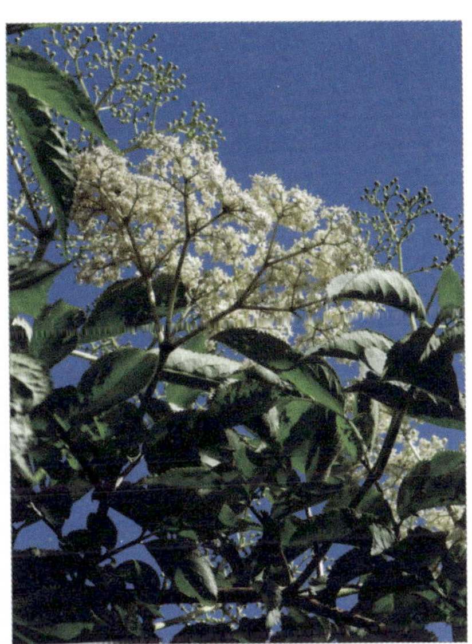

Start by drawing out two boxes side-by-side on the page with a pencil and ruler. Perhaps choose two photographs of your tree, one showing most of the structure for the white-on-black box, and the second zoomed in for more detail on the black-on-white box. Select the dimensions and aspect ratio of your box according to your reference photographs.

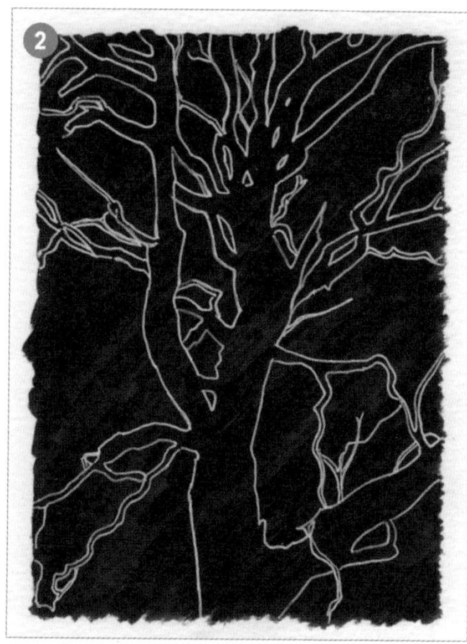

Frame 1: White on Black

❶ Using a black ink brush pen (or black ink and a paintbrush), fill in the box with ink, allowing your marks to overlap the straight lines and produce a roughly textured, brush-like edge. It doesn't matter if this ink painting is not uniform, in fact this can be exaggerated with spaces left between the brushstrokes if you prefer.

❷ Once the ink has fully dried, draw the outline of the tree's basic structure, the trunk and main branches, over the ink box with a white or pale-coloured gel pen. This is a great practice exercise for freehand drawing, although a faint, white coloured pencil outline could be used if you prefer to have the option of redrawing.

❸ Use a thinner gel pen to add further details such as twigs or leaves. You could add more detail to shade the trunk (see Gallery) or leave the tree shape as a simple line drawing.

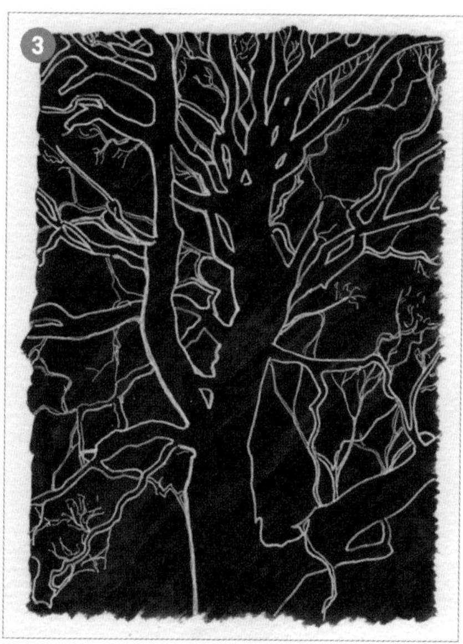

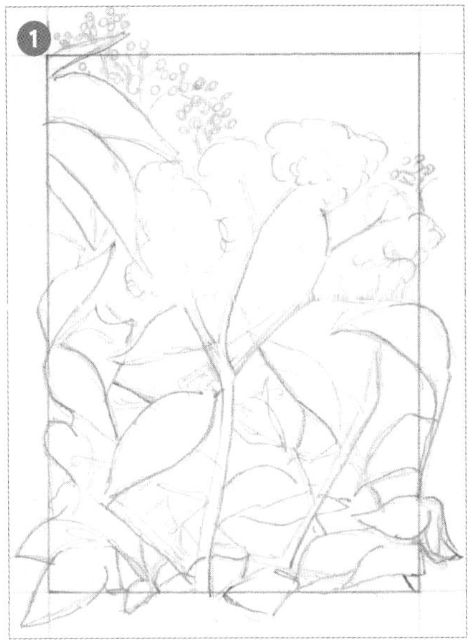

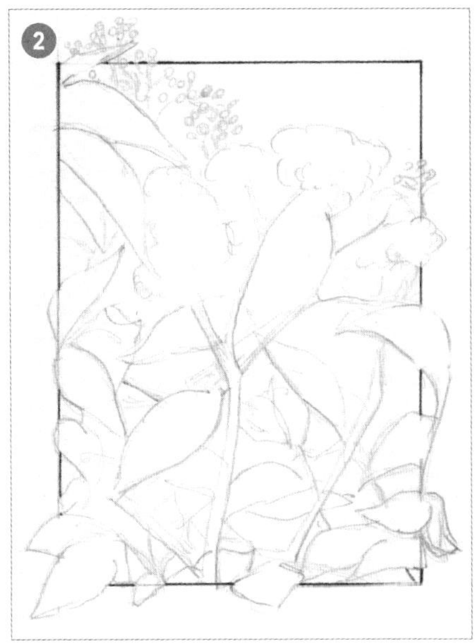

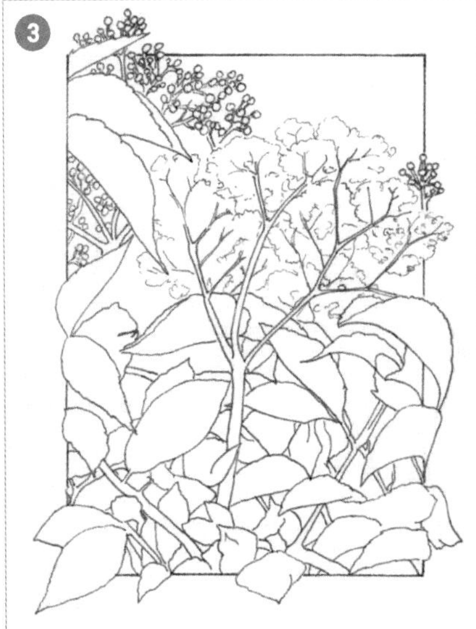

Frame 2: Black on White

❶ Begin with a graphite sketch, allowing some elements to overlap and extend beyond the box. Here, I drew some of the elderflower leaves and flowers emerging from the top left and escaping over the box at the bottom. In contrast, some parts of the drawing are strictly contained within the outline.

❷ Next, draw around the box with a fineliner and ruler, carefully excluding all of the parts of the drawing that have escaped over the frame.

❸ Finish outlining the rest of the graphite sketch, adding further details as you work. You could use a range of fineliner sizes to emphasise different parts of the subject. Remove the underlying pencil lines with a pointed or battery-operated eraser. Coloured pencil could be added at this stage, or leave the drawing as line art.

Gallery

The examples on this page take a slightly different approach. Further details and shading have been added, with squiggly lines of gel pen representing leaves on the black background in the example right, in contrast to the solid hatching used for the tree's structure. Similar contrasts of line suggest texture in the black-on-white drawing of the sweet chestnut in the example below.

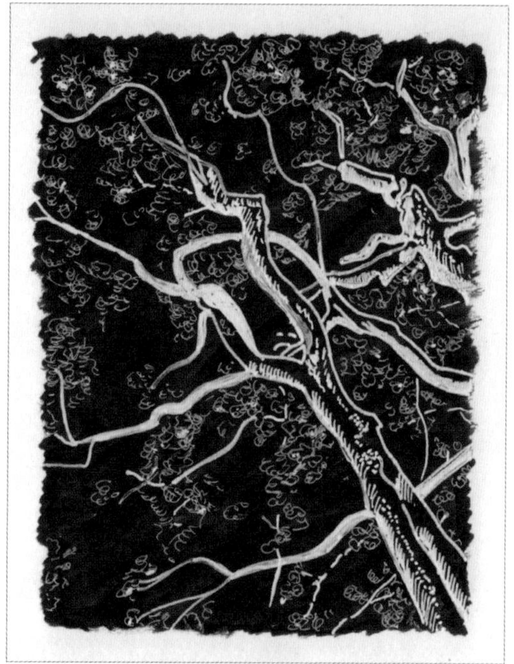

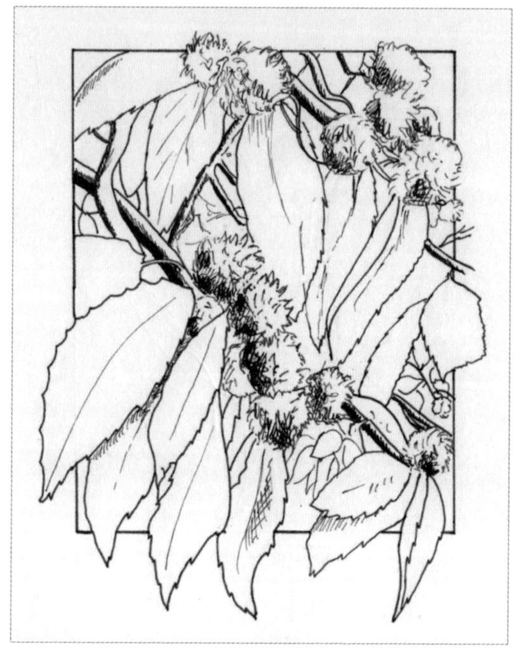

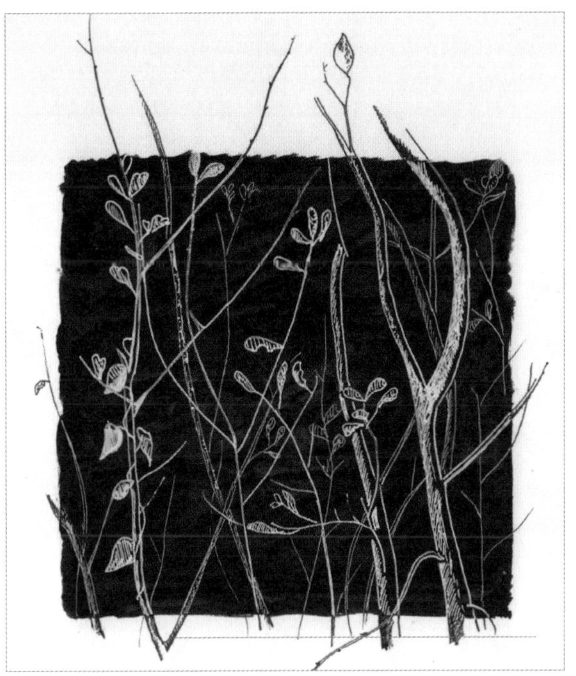

In these examples, the elements are "escaping" from the frame, which amplifies their impact. Note how the background landscape is contained within the frame in the example below, but the tree itself emerges dramatically towards the viewer, enhancing the perspective.

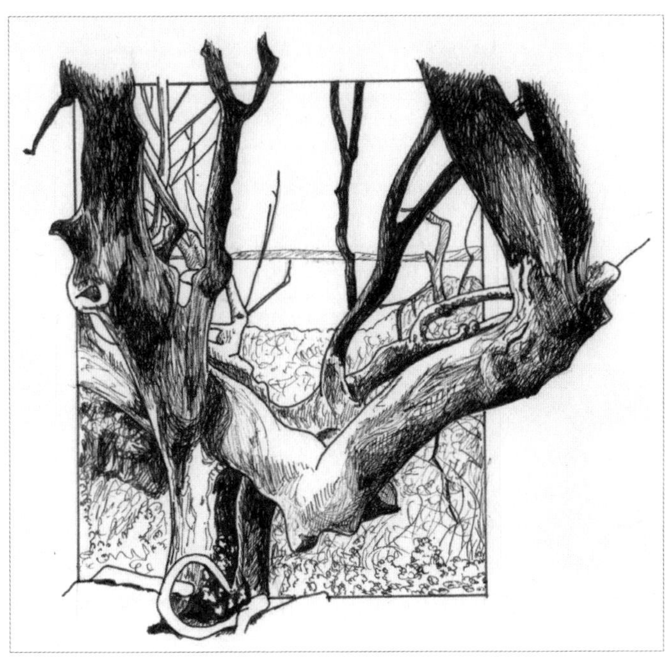

Lesson 16

Organic Collage

For the last exercise of the book, it is time to start incorporating the tree itself into your artwork, using leaf and flower pressings, together with gathered materials. Careful arrangements of your found or foraged pieces can rarely be beaten to summarise the perfection of nature.

Pressing is traditionally done between the pages of a large book, using blotting paper to protect the pages. A dedicated flower press could also be used. At least two weeks is recommended as minimum for effective pressing, although faster microwave-based methods are available.

The most important element of this form of collage is composition. Aim for plenty of negative space – the white space around solid shapes – and to emulate nature as much as you can. For example, there is little better than the careful layering of leaves produced by the downward branches of the tree itself. Take your cues from nature, using photographs and sketches as your guide.

Additional materials:

Scissors, collage materials, stubby paintbrush, EVA glue, paintbrush, paper tape, toned paper

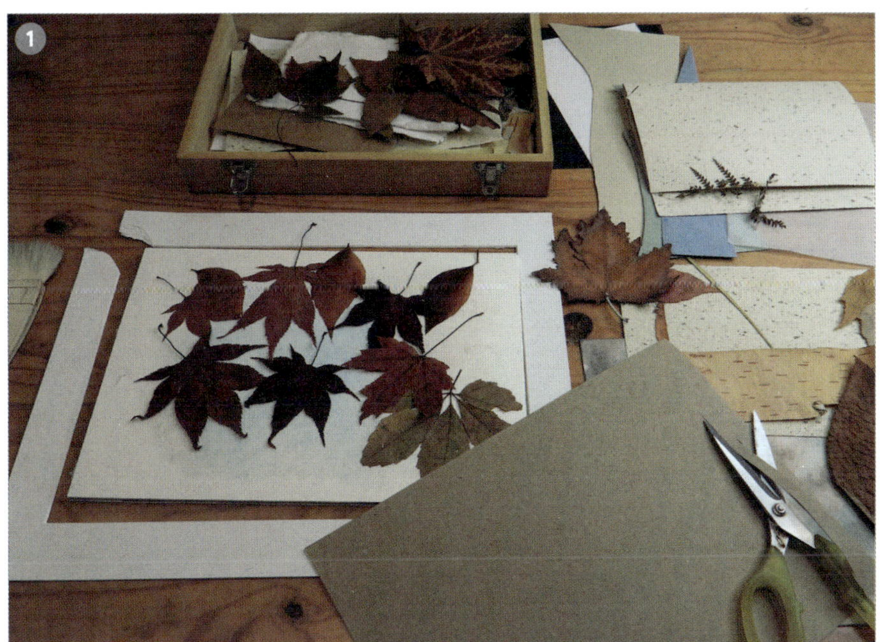

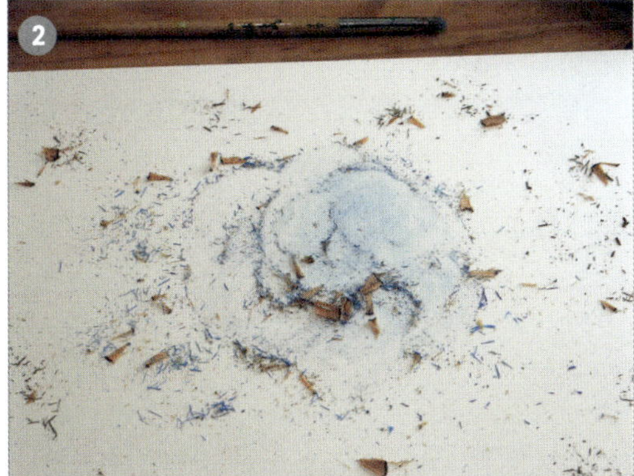

❶ Gather your dried materials (see Gathering, on the following page) and supporting textures. Have a range of different collage materials to hand to supplement your foraged pieces. This shows my desk laid out ready with the beginnings of a collage piece. Notice there are several different papers together with some scissors and my box of scraps.

❷ Prepare a background for your collage. In this example, I wanted a mainly white background but decided to add some soft coloured pencil using the pencil-sharpenings method described in Lesson 7.

Gathering

When gathering organic materials to include in your collage, it is important to consider the following:

Can I Take Material Without Damaging the Tree?
Autumn is a great time to gather fallen leaves from deciduous trees, or head out after a storm or municipal pruning to see what you can rescue from the ground. Be kind to paper bark trees; gather bark that has already been shed rather than pulling it from the trunk.

Is this Material Safe?
Check that the species of tree or plant that you are collecting does not have toxic or caustic sap, or other properties such as a sticky or staining residue. Go prepared with a field guide and gloves, and if in doubt, leave it be.

Ease of Pressing
Not all leaves are equal when it comes to pressing; for example, those with a highly glossy surface are more likely to brown and dry rather than press satisfactorily. A little experimentation may be needed to work out the best leaves for your area.

Storage
Once my leaves and flowers have all been pressed and removed from the flower press, I relocate them to a wooden box to keep them flat and dry. I also keep other interesting paper and organic scraps in here for collage purposes.

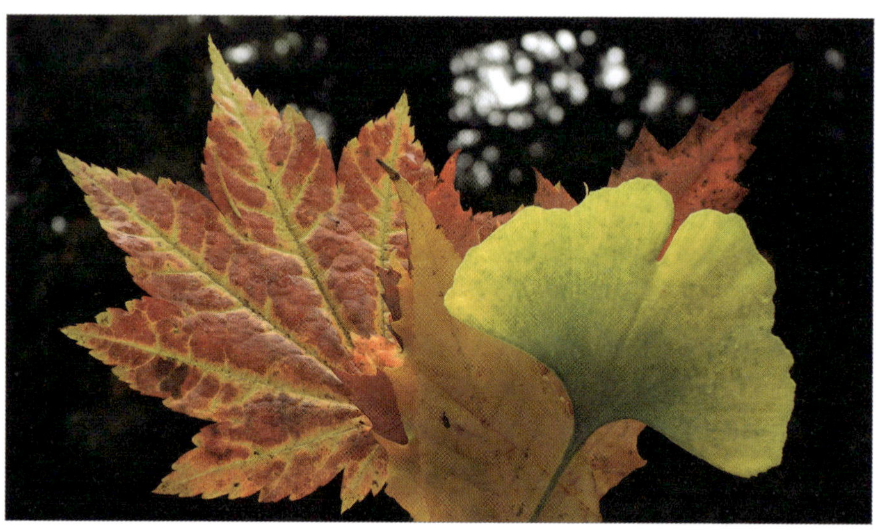

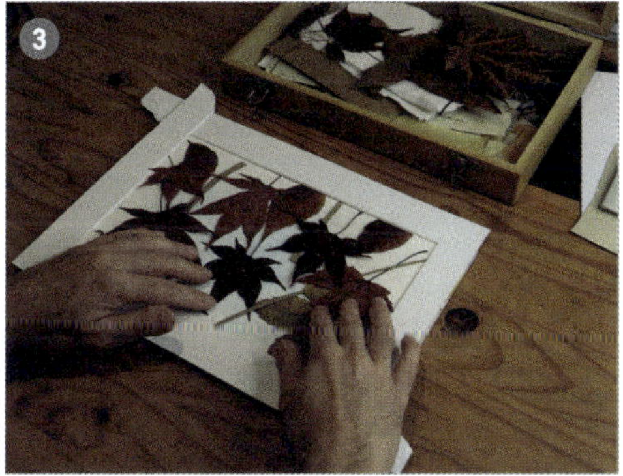

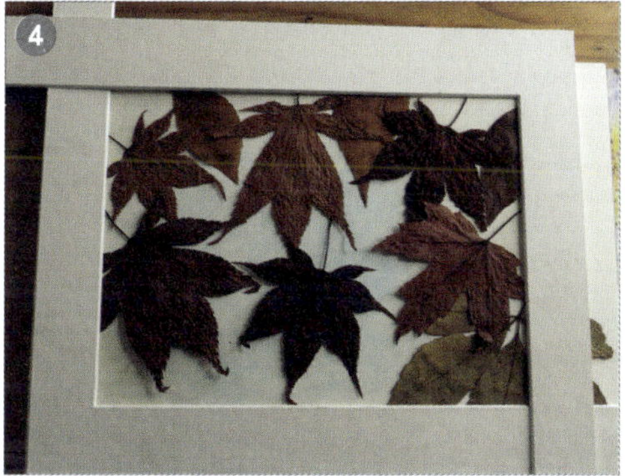

❸ Once your background is prepared, lay out a selection of your leaves and experiment with different layouts. It may take a few tries before you are happy with the positions of all your materials. I like to use an old frame mount to check the composition of my collage.

❹ Take photographs of every layout attempt that you like but continue to keep experimenting with new ideas to help you decide on a final composition. Keep this photograph to hand as a reference as you will now remove all but the bottom layer of materials.

❺ Begin by fixing the bottom layer of leaves and materials, using either EVA glue or soft tape. Use tape for stems and other areas that are tricky to glue. You can either hide this tape or make it into a feature. Strips of toned paper can be used in your composition to represent twigs and branches.

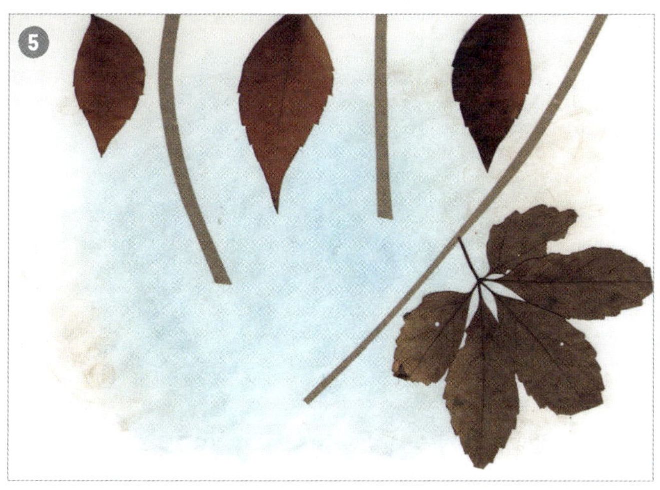

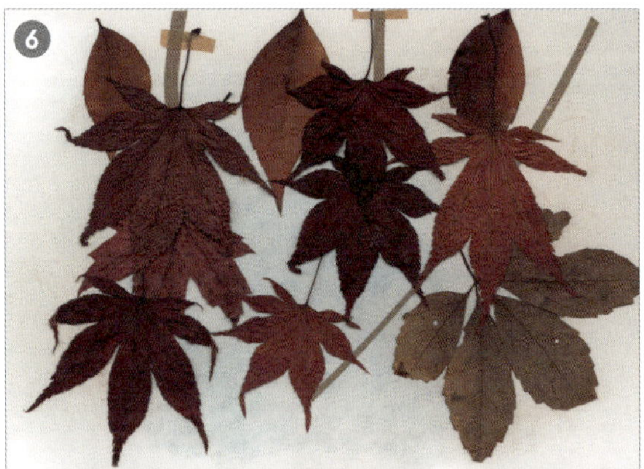

TIP:

Avoid painting glue over your picture itself to minimise marks in the negative spaces.

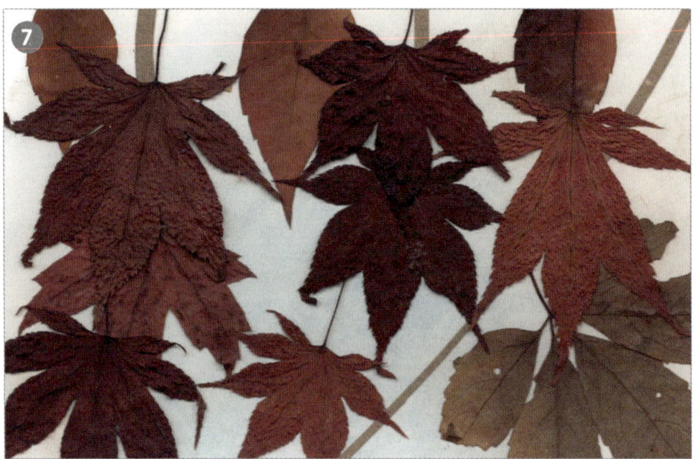

6 Continue to layer up your leaves and materials. Be careful with overlapping features, ensuring that they are well glued to avoid damaging the edges. Working on scrap paper, apply the glue onto the back of the item with a paintbrush, ensuring there is a good coating of glue right to the edge before transferring to the picture. If your leaves are relatively smooth, paint a layer of glue over the top of them to help seal in their colour.

7 Once complete, you may need to crop into the collage to achieve the desired final effect. This is best done using a frame mount or by digitising the image. Because of the short-term nature of organic collages, I usually scan them in and make prints from the final image. This makes cropping easy and retains the integrity of the artwork indefinitely.

Gallery

This example combines botanical inks (made from plants), handmade papers, brown paper tape, paper birch bark fragments, pressed leaves, pressed flowers, and brown paper strips into a pleasing composition. The central piece of paper creates a frame effect, inspired by the framed sketches in Lesson 15. Some elements were allowed to overlap the paper base. These were strengthened by gluing to another piece of paper stuck to the base of the artwork and then carefully cut out with a craft knife.

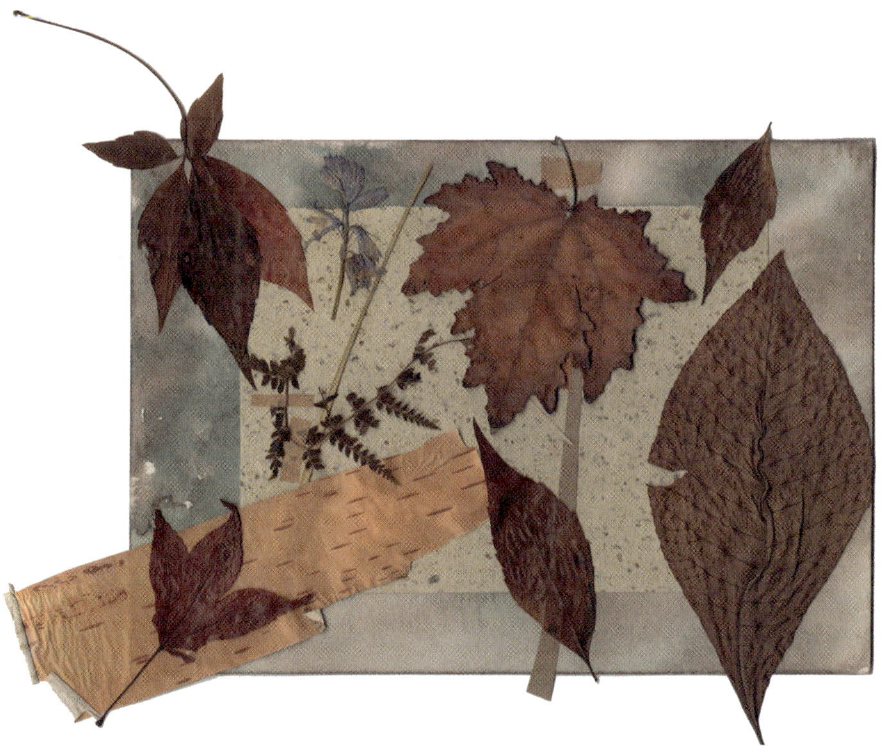

Nature Journaling

Nature journaling is the act of creatively recording your relationship with nature. There are no rules about how to keep a nature journal, what it should look like, and what materials you might use. If you have enjoyed nature journaling your tree, you might like to continue this activity and further explore the nature of your local area.

There are many ways to nature journal, but it is not always easy to start that first blank page. Below are three of my favourite prompts for starting nature journaling in any location. Open a page of your journal and let's start your first entry.

Meta Information

The first thing you need to do is write down the date, the time, and your location. Add a few observations about what the weather is doing right now and anything interesting about recent conditions. If you like (I do this regularly now), describe how you feel today in a few words too.

Prompt 1: What Else is Here?

Sit or stand in one location for at least 10 minutes. Close your eyes, open them, then write down the first thing you notice. Now ask yourself "what else is here?" The things you notice do not all have to be visual, perhaps there is an interesting sound or smell. Keep listing as long as you can. This is a great way to find some things of interest that you would like to explore further through writing, drawing, or identifying (see Identifying Species).

Prompt 2: A Curiosity Diagram

Do a drawing of something you find that interests you. The intention of this is not to make a good sketch, but to foster curiosity and to observe things more closely. Label the sketch with three things that made you take an interest in it in the first place. This could be a simple list or you might write questions. It's up to you whether you want to find the answers to your questions later on.

Prompt 3: The "Directions" Method

Do a sketch or write some observations for what is north/south/east/west of you, and/or what is above/below/left/right/ahead/behind you. This works well when combined with the other prompts. For example you could use a different type of idea for each direction – perhaps begin with a curiosity diagram of something you find on the ground, followed by a "what else is here?" list of everything you notice to your left.

The Nature Journaling Circle

If you're interested in learning more about nature journaling and continuing to advance your artistic skills under my tuition, take a look at www.naturejournalingcircle.com. This online art school and community provides:

- *Courses and tutorials on nature journaling and art techniques.*
- *Monthly live tutorial and social chats via Zoom.*
- *A growing on-demand library of all past tutorial content.*
- *Motivation to keep journaling, with templates, resources, and monthly prompts.*
- *A friendly journal-sharing community forum.*

Join in with a monthly or annual membership, by purchasing an on-demand course, or by joining the community sharing space for free. We would love to see your creations inspired by the lessons in this book!

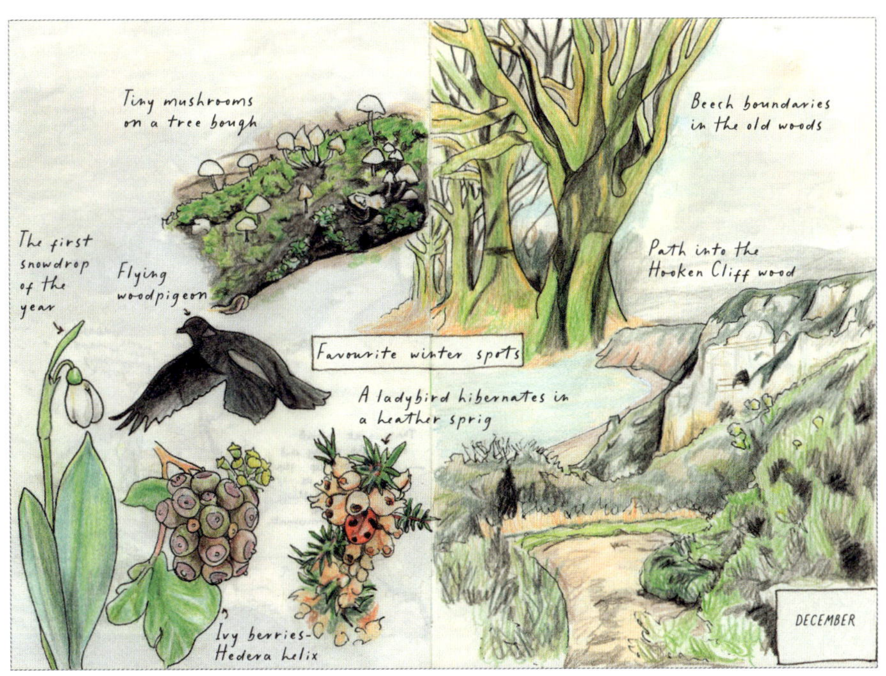

Identifying Species

Over the years, I have developed a creativity-forward process for reaching a species identification. This method is designed to be slow and thoughtful, with the intention of mindful learning rather than reaching a quick answer. Use this method as often as you can, and you will find that the species names will stay with you for longer. You can add these notes to your nature journal, or create a separate species field book of your own.

Step 1: Sketch, Sample, and Photograph

First, gather as much information as you can in the field. Look for distinguishing features to notice. For a tree this might be leaf shape, canopy shape, and whether leaves alternate in their positions on the stem or are in pairs or clusters. Sketch any fruits, nuts, or flowers present or the shape of the buds on a deciduous tree in winter. Also note whether there are other trees of the same type close by or whether this specimen is isolated, and describe the features of the environment. You can use a similar sketching and questioning approach for other types of organism, such as flowering plants or bird life. Finally, take photographs and any samples you can without damaging the subject.

Step 2: Use a Guidebook

A good nature guidebook or field guide is a fantastic resource. There are thousands of localised and subject-specific guidebooks available, so here are a few tips on finding a good reference book:

- Choose a relatively recent edition as species names can and often do change; more recent editions often include changes in distribution as a result of climate change or biodiversity losses.
- Check that the guidebook is suitable for your region; often a more localised book is more useful than a general guide to global or continental species.
- The choice between photos or illustrations is a matter of personal preference. Illustrations are often better as they isolate important features, although photos may allow for a more immediate comparison.
- Be aware that most guidebooks are limited in scope and are just one stage in this investigation. For example, trees can often be imported or naturalised exotics, and may not appear in regional guidebooks, so wider research may be needed.

Step 3: Internet and Apps

Identification apps can be incredibly helpful in our search for a species identification and they will often result in a quick answer. However, since responses are immediate, it is tempting to allow apps to become the only stage in the identification process. Try not to let this happen, at least not all the time. See Resources for a few app suggestions.

The internet is also really useful. Image searches can be used to compare similar species with your records, or to get further photographs based on a guess from a guidebook. Sometimes, typing keywords such as "tree, yellow flowers, pointed leaves" into a search engine can produce useful websites to help narrow down your search.

Step 4: Got Your Result? Don't Stop There!

Knowing the species name is only the first step in getting to know a species. Guidebooks and internet searches open up worlds of information. Archival, herbal, foraging, and folk histories are just as interesting as scientific data. Get stuck in: perhaps you can use this extra information to annotate your sketches.

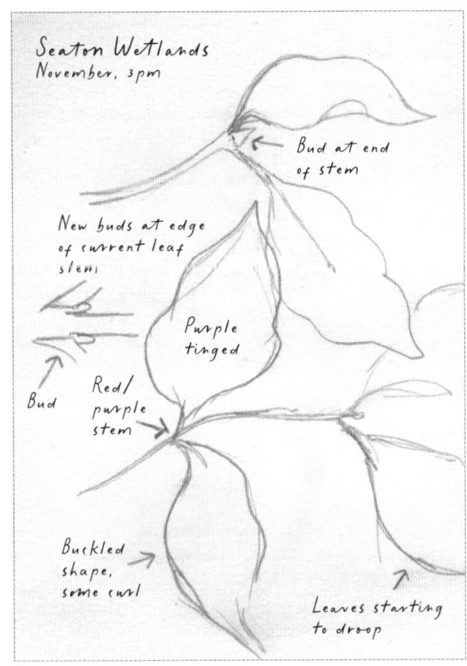

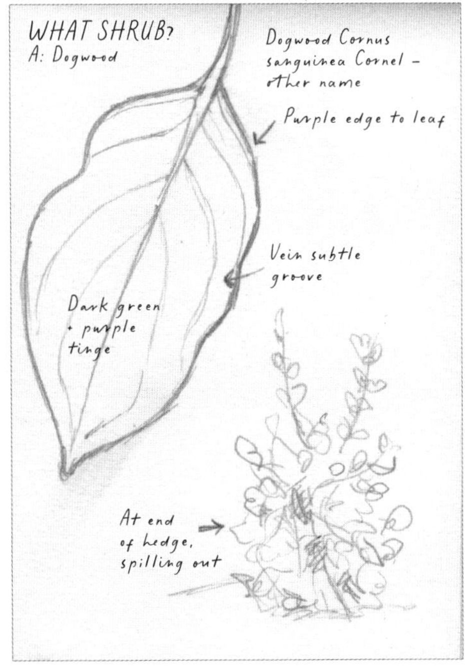

TIP:

Scribble down a big question mark or ask a question such as "What tree?" in your journal, perhaps in a different colour. This will remind you to answer the question later.

Art in Stewardship

One of the greatest effects of creativity in nature, together with improved wellbeing, is the enriched love and respect that we feel for the locations that we observe in detail. Love grows from intimate knowledge of a species or place, and we naturally want to protect the things that we love.

If getting to know your tree or location has affected you in this way, think about how you can give back. A life-drawing artist will usually pay their sitter, so how can we repay our tree or woodland for all the inspiration it has given us through this project? Below are a few ideas from my own practice, but be creative and ask around – there may be some other way you can help.

Volunteer

Many woods, parks, and nature reserves will have an active volunteer group. You might be enlisted to help with weeding or invasive species clearance, building fences or paths, or pruning or other maintenance. If you have expertise you could offer, such as writing, organisational, or graphic design skills, you might be able to help on the administrative side of an organisation's activities.

Donate

If you cannot donate your time, perhaps consider a regular donation to a tree-focused charity. Some such charities circulate wonderful educational materials to their members and may have tree-focused events, too.

Inspire Others

One of the ultimate ways to give back is to inspire the same love for nature in others. If you are willing, share your tree project widely and let your enthusiasm catch on. If you are particularly keen, you might organise an exhibition or a community project. An outdoor sketching or walking group is a great way to inspire others and meet new friends. Don't underestimate the potential impacts of sharing your work online, on social media, or writing or speaking about how nature has positively affected your life.

Be the Change

If you are not a loud talker, a big sharer, or someone with time or money to spare, there are other ways to give back! The simplest is to love and care for nature in our daily lives. All the little things – recycling, consuming less, and so on – are important, together with simply taking a moment to actually notice and appreciate that nature is here, all around us.

Documenting Nature's Story

A few years ago, I was working on an art piece based on one very special tree. I returned to the tree every few weeks and recorded how it changed as the season shifted from winter to spring. I sketched the tree's branches and leaves. I looked at the overall shape of the tree from several different angles and examined the other life it supported. I also researched the tree's species and looked into current and old maps of the area surrounding it, imagining reasons for its shape and position. The day before the work was due to be exhibited, a storm blew through the town, with strong winds from the opposite direction to normal. That day, my beloved old tree lost most of its uppermost branches and its shape was changed forever.

Though unplanned, the resulting artwork now represents the last few months in the final phase of this tree's life. As artists and nature lovers, we have a unique opportunity to document the changes in the world around us at this critical time for nature. How many more important moments can be captured by engaged nature artists as the world changes?

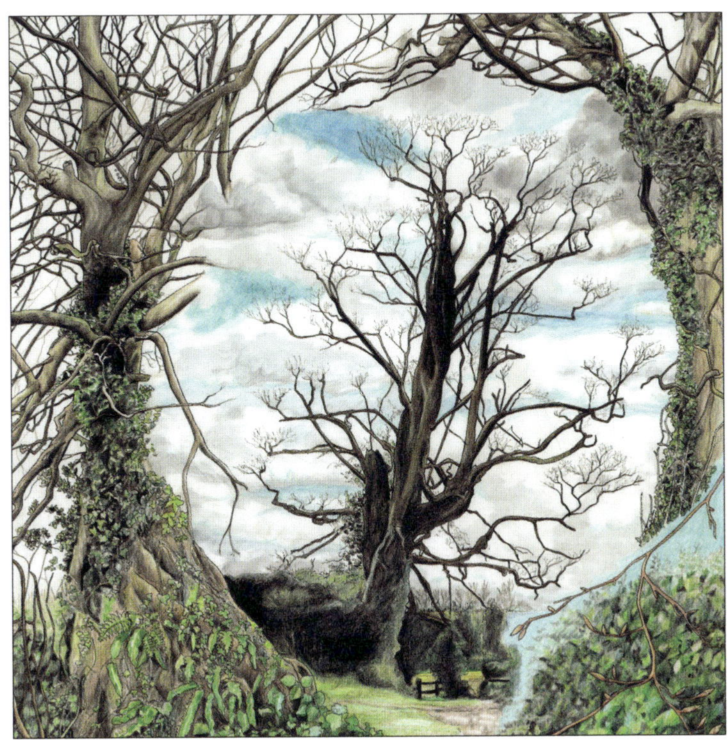

Resources

Nature Journaling

The Wild Wonder Foundation – An excellent resource for nature journalers and nature journaling teachers worldwide. www.wildwonder.org

International Nature Journaling Week – This week-long, international initiative runs every year in the first week of June. www.naturejournalingweek.com

Journaling with Nature – This excellent website and podcast features nature journals from all around the world. www.journalingwithnature.com

Identification Apps

Pay attention to an app's certainty ratings. These platforms run on artificial intelligence and are not always correct!

iNaturalist and iNaturalist Seek (International) – These great apps allow you to join a community of enthusiastic recorders of nature.

Merlin (International) – Imagine you could find out which bird is singing as you stand outside in nature... you can with this amazing app.

ObsIdentify (UK and Europe) – An excellent app for all manner of wildlife and plant identification.

Google Lens (International) – Designed to identify all sorts of different things, not just wildlife, but can be useful in a pinch!

Tree Organisations

These are just a few of the hundreds of amazing tree-focused organisations around the world. Seek out further international, national, or local organisations to support.

Woodland Trust
www.woodlandtrust.org.uk

Arbor Day Foundation
www.arborday.org

Rainforest Trust
www.rainforesttrust.org

Greening Australia
www.greeningaustralia.org.au

Royalty-Free Reference Photos

It can be very helpful to have access to additional photos to support your artistic development, although I recommend that these are only used as a supplementary resource (in addition to your own photos and explorations) rather than your only source of inspiration!

Pixabay – www.pixabay.com

Pexels – www.pexels.com

You can find all the reference photographs used in the lessons here: www.flickr.com/photos/alexboonart

Bibliography

Understanding Trees

Gooley, Tristan, *How to Read a Tree* (London, 2023)

Hemery, Gabriel and Simblet, Sarah, *The New Sylva* (London, 2021)

Simard, Suzanne, *Finding the Mother Tree* (London, 2022)

Wohlleben, Peter, *The Heartbeat of Trees* (Glasgow, 2022)

Wohlleben, Peter, *The Hidden Life of Trees* (Glasgow, 2017)

Nature Journaling and Art Skills

Blockley, Ann, *Poetic Woods* (London, 2023)

Foxon, Ali, *The Green Sketching Handbook* (London, 2022)

Hollender, Wendy, *Botanical Drawing in Color* (New York, 2010)

Laws, John Muir, *The Laws Guide to Nature Drawing and Journaling* (Berkeley, 2016)

Sutherland, Dianne, *Sketching Nature* (David and Charles, 2025)

Walker Leslie, Claire, *Keeping a Nature Journal* (New York, 2021)

Further Inspiration

There are hundreds of illustrated nature books on my shelves – in fact, collecting older, often out of print, editions of nature journals and naturalist's sketchbooks is a bit of a hobby of mine! There are many, many books I could mention, but here are just a few of my absolute favourites that have greatly influenced my work and that I hope will inspire you too.

Baty, Patrick, *Nature's Palette* (London, 2021)

Bilclough, Annemarie (Ed.), *Beatrix Potter: Drawn to Nature* (London, 2021)

Brown, Jo, *Secrets of a Devon Wood* (London, 2020)

Hockney, David and Gayford, Martin, *Spring Cannot Be Cancelled* (Stoke-on-Trent, 2022)

Hoffman, Mary Jo, *Still: The Art of Noticing* (New York, 2024)

Holden, Edith, *The Country Diary of an Edwardian Lady* (London, 1977)

MacFarlane, Robert and Morris, Jackie, *The Lost Words* (London, 2017)

Oliver, Mary, *A Thousand Mornings* (London, 2018)

About the Author

Alex Boon is an artist and nature journaling educator. He studied environmental science to PhD level before deciding to leave academia and move to the countryside. He spends his days wandering the wild places, documenting nature in words and sketches, and sharing what he finds on YouTube, Instagram, and with his Nature Journaling Circle community. His greatest joy is inspiring other people to get into nature and helping them to explore their creativity. His biggest inspirations are Edith Holden, Beatrix Potter, Flora Thompson, and Jackie Morris. When he isn't drawing or exploring nature, he enjoys playing piano and doing ashtanga yoga. He lives by the sea with his partner Davey and their beloved cat, Luna.

For more about Alex visit www.alexboonart.com or follow @alexboonart on Instagram and YouTube.

Acknowledgements

As a first-time author-illustrator, I greatly appreciate the opportunity given by Nigel Browning and the team at David & Charles to produce not just one but two nature art books! Thank you to Katie Hardwicke for helping to smooth out the text and to the design team for turning a portfolio loaded with drawings into the book you hold in your hands. I would like to thank Devon Artist Network for providing me with the encouragement of a bursary award and a session with the excellent photographer Jim Wileman, whose beautiful photos have been included in this book. Thanks are also due to Davey Atkinson, Anna Brewster, and Steve Boon for support through the process of creating these books, and all the Nature Journaling Circle community members for believing in me and helping to build an online space for mindful outdoor creativity.

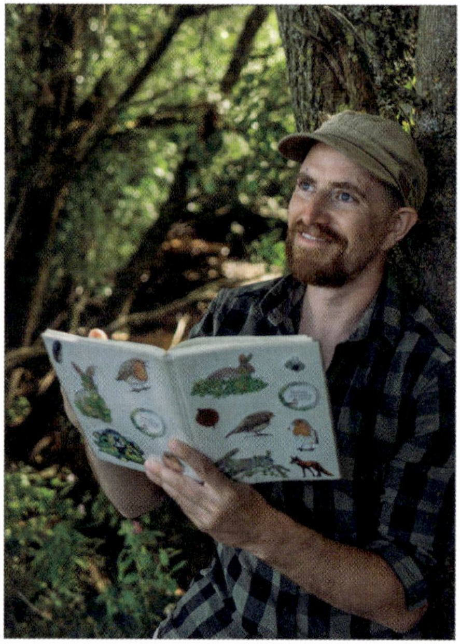

Index

A DAVID AND CHARLES BOOK

David and Charles is an imprint of David and Charles, Ltd, Suite A, Tourism House, Pynes Hill, Exeter, EX2 5WS

First published in the UK and USA in 2025

A catalogue record for this book is available from the British Library.

ISBN-13: 9781446314791 hardback
ISBN-13: 9781446314838 EPUB

This book has been printed on paper from approved suppliers and made from pulp from sustainable sources.

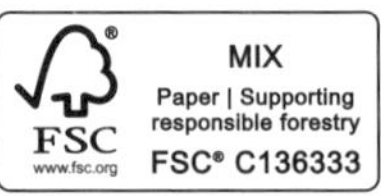

Printed in China by Asia Pacific Offset for:
David and Charles, Ltd, Suite A, Tourism House, Pynes Hill, Exeter, EX2 5WS

10 9 8 7 6 5 4 3 2 1

Publishing Director: Ame Verso
Commissioning Editor: Nigel Browning
Publishing Manager: Jeni Chown
Editor: Jessica Cropper
Project Editor: Katie Hardwicke
Lead Designer: Sam Staddon
Designers: Nikki Ellis & Jess Pearson
Pre-press Designer: Susan Reansbury
Illustrations: Alex Boon
Photography: Alex Boon
Anna Brewster (page 7)
Jim Wileman (page 126)
Production Manager: Beverley Richardson

David and Charles publishes high-quality books on a wide range of subjects. For more information visit www.davidandcharles.com.

Share your art with us on social media using #dandcbooks and follow us on Facebook and Instagram by searching for @dandcbooks.

Layout of the digital edition of this book may vary depending on reader hardware and display settings.